Advice to Writers

Advice
to Writers

A Compendium of Quotes,
Anecdotes, and Writerly Wisdom
From a Dazzling Array
of Literary Lights

COMPILED AND EDITED BY

Jon Winokur

PANTHEON BOOKS
NEW YORK

All rights reserved under International and Pan-American Copyright
Conventions. Published in the United States by Pantheon Books,
a division of Random House, Inc., New York, and simultaneously
in Canada by Random House of Canada Limited, Toronto.

Pantheon Books and colophon are registered trademarks of
Random House, Inc.

Library of Congress Cataloging-in-Publication Data

Advice to writers / compiled and edited by Jon Winokur.
     p.   cm.
    Includes index.
    ISBN 0-679-44387-8
    I. Authorship—Quotations, maxims, etc.   2. Authors—Quotations.
  I. Winokur, Jon.
  PN165.A385   1999
  808'.02—dc21   98-49030
                                              CIP

Random House Web Address: www.randomhouse.com

Book design by Deborah Kerner

Printed in the United States of America

First Edition
9 8 7 6 5 4 3 2 1

Contents

Acknowledgments

I'm grateful to all the writers, editors, literary agents, and booksellers who have dispensed advice about the writing life. I'm especially indebted to my faithful correspondents, who contributed freely, and for free. This book would not exist without their generosity.

Introduction

This book will not teach you how to write. Whether you use a fountain pen or a word processor, writing is finally sitting alone in a room and wrenching it out of yourself, and nobody can teach you that.

But you can learn, because writing is self-generating, one of the few skills you can acquire *from a book*—an otherwise pejorative phrase. Combined with a lot of trial and error: You don't just immerse yourself in books and then suddenly emerge a writer. You have to practice, because the writing muscle needs regular exercise, and no pain, no gain. There will be false starts and dead ends and self-doubt, but you don't have to go to Iowa or Bread Loaf, and you don't need a writing teacher. You need teachers.

You learn to write from other writers, from reading their novels, poetry, plays, biographies. But you have to read like a writer. A civilian reads for entertainment, information, solace. A writer reads for all these, and for craft and technique and tricks of the trade. A writer reads critically, noting what works and what doesn't, silently cheering the arabesques and booing the clunkers, quibbling about the choice of a word here and the use of a semicolon there, always judging. In a way it's a curse: A writer never gets lost in a book, never surrenders to a text, never fully suspends disbelief, because a writer is always watching, even when he's reading.

The sixteenth-century French writer Michel de Montaigne, the inventor of the modern essay, once remarked that "there are more books upon books than upon all other subjects." It's still true. In addition to models to emulate, there are all kinds of books upon books: how to find a publisher, how to do research, how to prepare a manuscript. From Judith Appelbaum's indispensable *How to Get Happily Published*, to the venerable *Elements of Style* and *Paris Review Interviews*, to such modern classics as Anne Lamott's *Bird by Bird* and Richard Rhodes's *How to Write*, these books instruct, inspire, and feed—but never quite satisfy—an intense curiosity about the process of making literature.

And you can learn straight from the masters, because writers love to give advice, to colleagues and tyros alike. Down the centuries they've carried on a lively discussion of their craft, much of which is preserved in print. They share their hard-earned knowledge about everything from how to write dialogue to how to behave on television. They reveal trade secrets, they declare rules and commandments, and they expose the creative process. Here are samples of that writerly wisdom—pithy pronouncements and brief readings on the art of writing—from their rooms to your room.

J. W.
Pacific Palisades, California

Author's Note

Most of these quotations are from writers, but there are also contributions from a number of booksellers, editors, and publishing executives. And please note that I've quoted "writers" and not "authors." For me, an author is anyone who has published a book, while the word "writer" carries a value judgment. A writer is an artist, someone who writes out of the gut. A writer is something you *are*, whereas "author" refers to something you *do*. Almost anyone can be an author, from anthologists to autobiographers, diet doctors to financial gurus. Authors are a dime a dozen. Writers are rare.

Advice to Writers

Agents

Get an agent. Make no excuses for the failure to do so. Get an agent. Otherwise you're a babe among wolves.

Brendan Francis

It is more difficult to get a qualified literary agent than it is to get a publishing contract.

John Boswell

First of all, you must have an agent, and in order to get a good one, you must have sold a considerable amount of material. And in order to sell a considerable amount of material, you must have an agent. Well, you get the idea.

Steve McNeil

Most large trade publishers return unsolicited manuscripts unread or scarcely glanced at.... Publishers that refuse to read slush generally return manuscripts with printed notices stating that the firm reviews only submissions made by literary agents. In effect, agents have become the slush pile readers of the publishing industry.

Richard Curtis

Even the greenest of [Hollywood] agents serve a tremendously valuable function—since very few people in the business will read a script that is unrepresented, because of legal reasons.

William Goldman

My advice on dealing with publishers: Let your agent do it. Agents are more important than publishers. Agents are more important than anyone. Which brings me to my advice on dealing with agents. You can't. They won't speak to you. They're too important.

P. J. O'Rourke

Agents make good partners, particularly if you don't live in New York (but even if you do). If they're competent they know the going rates and the best terms; they know which editors might be interested in your work. Don't ask them for literary judgments about your projects. They'll give them and you'll be sorry you asked. (My agent friends will kill me for saying so, but literary acumen ain't their forte. Nor should it be—that's your job.) They'll cost you at least ten, more usually fifteen percent of your writing income. You should see as you go along that their contribution of contacts and negotiating expertise adds at least that much to the total (and if it doesn't add more, you ought to look elsewhere).

Richard Rhodes

Choose your agent as carefully as you would choose your accountant or lawyer. Or dentist.

Russell Banks

Choosing an agent is a lot like choosing a hairdresser. If you know a bunch of writers (and most writers do because who else is home all day?) ask the successful ones who represents them. If you don't know any writers, look at books by authors you admire and see which agent the author thanked in the acknowledgements. Send five to ten of these agents a résumé, cover letter, and proposal for what you're trying to sell (it's imperative that the prospective agent knows that you have a money-making project in mind). Interview the agents who respond positively and pick the one you like best. If no one responds positively, send your stuff to another five to ten agents. Don't take it personally. Think of it as practice in handling rejection. (Believe me, you'll need all the practice you can get.)

Margo Kaufman

Your agent is your lifeline, your reality check, and your best friend.

Rita Mae Brown

If you get an agent for your book, don't call him or her every day. When there is news, you will be the first to know.

Bill Adler

The only advice I have to give a young novelist is to fuck a really good agent.

John Cheever

Characters

When writing a novel a writer should create living people; people, not characters. A *character* is a caricature.

Ernest Hemingway

Begin with an individual and you find that you have created a type; begin with a type and you find that you have created—nothing.

F. Scott Fitzgerald

You can never know enough about your characters.

W. Somerset Maugham

Trollope said, "On the last day of each month recorded, every person in a work of fiction should be a month older than on the first." We go with our characters wherever they lead us, and as time makes its mark on us, so it must on them.

Hallie Burnett

I always pulp my acquaintances before serving them up. You would never recognize a pig in a sausage.

Frances Trollope

You must be very careful how you introduce your characters. The star plan is to talk about them before they appear so as to make the audience curious to see them, and sufficiently informed about them to save them the trouble of explaining their circumstance. But as some of the characters must open the play and cannot be prepared in this way, you must either fall back on the Parisian well-made play formula and begin with a conversation between the butler and housemaid or else start the characters with a strongly assertive scene, like *Richard III.*

George Bernard Shaw

It is a psychological trait in human nature that interest is established in the persons whom the playwright introduces at the beginning of his play so firmly that if the interest is then switched off to other persons who enter upon the scene later, a sense of disappointment ensues.

W. Somerset Maugham

The bad novelist constructs his characters; he directs them and makes them speak. The true novelist listens to them and watches them act; he hears their voices even before he knows them.

André Gide

If you want your reader to understand something about a given character, his habits of intellection and control of his emotions, show the reader what the character thinks about, and then the reader will think about it too.

George V. Higgins

Nothing is as important as a likeable narrator. Nothing holds a story together better.

Ethan Canin

A character is never a whole person, but just those parts of him that fit the story or the piece of writing. So the act of selection is the writer's first step in delineating character. From what does he select? From a whole mass of what Bernard De Voto used to call, somewhat clinically, "placental material." He must know an enormous amount more about each of his characters than he will ever use directly—childhood, family background, religion, schooling, health, wealth, sexuality, reading, tastes, hobbies—an endless questionnaire for the writer to fill out. For example, the writer knows that people speak, and therefore his characters will describe themselves indirectly when they talk. Clothing is a means of characterization. In short, each character has a style of his own in everything he does. These need not all be listed, but the writer should have a sure grasp of them. If he has, his characters will, within the book, read like people.

William Sloane

AFTER GRADUATING from Johns Hopkins in 1947 I began working for the *Baltimore Sun*. Elliott Coleman had steered me to the job. Elliott had come to Hopkins the previous fall to teach writing. He was a poet, a tall willowy man, prematurely white-haired, with a slightly fey manner and the great writing teacher's gift, which was to identify an ounce of quality in a ton of verbal trash and encourage the student to mine it. When I met him I was enamored of Ernest Hemingway, like almost everyone else in his course, and ground out story after story about sardonic fellows sitting in bars before trudging off to brutal ends. After reading a hundred stories like this, Elliott, who wanted us to discover Marcel Proust, threw up his hands in class one day, cried, "Hemingway's swell, but he's out! out!" and strode from the room.

Even in my embarrassing Hemingway imitations, however, he found something to encourage. "You write dialogue extremely well," he said. It wasn't true, but he'd identified my one skill that might be worth developing. The encouragement kept me from dropping the class. Still, my characters remained hard types who lumbered off to defeat or death with stoic resignation. After laboring through a dozen such tales, Elliott gave me one of the most valuable suggestions I'd ever had about writing.

"Don't you think it would make your tough guys a little more interesting to the reader if once in a while you had one bend down to smell a rose?" he asked.

Russell Baker

A novelist's characters must be with him as he lies down to sleep, and as he wakes from his dreams. He must learn to hate them and to love them.

Anthony Trollope

Front-rank characters should have some defect, some conflicting inner polarity, some real or imagined inadequacy.

Barnaby Conrad

I would never write about someone who is not at the end of his rope.

Stanley Elkin

The protagonist of a play cannot be a perfect person. If he were, he could not improve, and he must come out at the end of the play a more admirable human being than he went in.

Maxwell Anderson

The character that lasts is an ordinary guy with some extraordinary qualities.

Raymond Chandler

A character, to be acceptable as more than a chess piece, has to be ignorant of the future, unsure about the past, and not at all sure of what he's supposed to be doing.

Anthony Burgess

When I used to teach creative writing, I would tell the students to make their characters want something right away—even if it's only a glass of water. Characters paralyzed by the meaninglessness of modern life still have to drink water from time to time.

Kurt Vonnegut

The characters have their own lives and their own logic, and you have to act accordingly.

Isaac Bashevis Singer

A character has his own logic. He goes his way, one goes with him; he has some perceptions, one perceives them with him. You do him justice; you don't grind your own axe.

Saul Bellow

TOLSTOY SAID a great thing [about characterization]: You can tell that a marriage is on the rocks when they speak to each other rationally.

David Mamet

"Character is Fate," said Heraclitus in 500 B.C. or thereabouts. But "Our characters are the result of our conduct," added Aristotle a hundred years or so later. We will find character and action even more inseparably entwined in fiction than they appear to be in life.

Rust Hills

Naming your characters Aristotle and Plato is not going to make their relationship interesting unless you make it so on the page.

Annie Dillard

Names are terribly important. I spend forever coming up with names. Sometimes a character doesn't work until I change his name. In *Bandits,* Frank Matusi didn't work. I changed him to Jack Delaney and suddenly he opened up.

Elmore Leonard

If you're silent for a long time, people just arrive in your mind.

Alice Walker

You put a character out there and you're in their power. You're in trouble if they're in yours.

Ann Beattie

That trite little whimsy about characters getting out of hand; it is as old as the quills. My characters are galley slaves.

Vladimir Nabokov

The legend that characters run away from their authors—taking up drugs, having sex operations, and becoming president—implies that the writer is a fool with no knowledge or mastery of his craft.

The idea of authors running around helplessly behind their cretinous inventions is contemptible.

John Cheever

The moment comes when a character does or says something you hadn't thought about. At that moment he's alive and you leave it to him.

Graham Greene

By the end, you should be inside your character, actually operating from within somebody else, and knowing him pretty well, as that person knows himself or herself. You're sort of a predator, an invader of people.

William Trevor

If you want to know your characters better, ask yourself: "How would they behave in a quarrel?"

Barnaby Conrad

I don't like to throw characters into a plot as though it were a raging torrent where they are swept along. What interests me are the complications and nuances of character. Few of my characters are described externally; we see them from the inside out.

Michael Ondaatje

My characters are quite as real to me as so-called real people; which is one reason why I'm not subject to what is known as loneliness. I have plenty of company.

William S. Burroughs

Colleagues

I've always had a feeling it's *dangerous* to be friends with a writer. . . .
you can end up talking away your books.

Norman Mailer

The fewer writers you know the better.

Maeve Brennan

There are two kinds of writers: hustlers and sanctimonious
hustlers.

Edward Hoagland

In 1967, when I was twenty, I wrote an—inevitably—earnest first
novel. I showed my efforts to the only published writer I knew. He
was kind enough to write a long critique, a largely charitable assess-
ment in which he expounded upon the challenges of first person
narration, the difficulties of the picaresque style, and the need for
consistency in fictional point of view. He allowed that some of my
characters were effective, was indulgent with my attempts at plot
development, and even went so far as to say, "the thing as a whole
is rather likable." But, at the end of his commentary, he appended
this postscript: "It has just occurred to me that there is, however,
the dreadful possibility that your book is supposed to be serious."

P. J. O'Rourke

Keep away from books and from men who get their ideas from books, and your own books will always be fresh.

George Bernard Shaw

To choose a writer for a friend is like palling around with your cardiologist, who might be musing as you talk to him that you are a sinking man. A writer's love for another writer is never quite free of malice.

Anatole Broyard

BEST ADVICE I ever got was from the Romanian poet Nichita Stanescu, who told me in Bucharest, before I emigrated: "Learn English. French is dead."

Andrei Codrescu

Fine writers should split hairs together, and sit side by side, like friendly apes, to pick the fleas from each other's prose.

Logan Pearsall Smith

Artists never thrive in colonies. Ants do. What the budding artist needs is the privilege of wrestling with his problems in solitude— and now and then a piece of red meat.

Henry Miller

....

For Christ sake write and don't worry what the boys will say nor whether it will be a masterpiece nor what. I write one page of masterpiece to ninety one pages of shit. I try to put the shit in the waste-basket. . . . Forget your personal tragedy. We are all bitched from the start and you especially have to be hurt like hell before you can write seriously.

Ernest Hemingway,
IN A LETTER TO **F. Scott Fitzgerald** (1934)

....

After suggesting [that young writers] look into *The Writer's Chapbook* I recommend they keep a diary, at least a page a day, and faithfully, and also to get into the habit of letter writing to other writers. The advantages that come with doing this seem obvious—both are exercises which hone the communicative skills.

George Plimpton

I WAS Sinclair Lewis's secretary-chess-opponent-chauffeur-protégé back when I was 24, and he told me sternly that if I could be anything else be it, but if I HAD to be a writer, I might make it. He also said, as he threw away the first 75 expository pages of my first novel: "People read fiction for emotion—not information."

Barnaby Conrad

There are other writers who would persuade you not to go on, that everything is nonsense, that you should kill yourself. They, of course, go on to write another book while you have killed yourself.

John Gardner

Critics and Criticism

Listen carefully to first criticisms of your work. Note just what it is about your work that critics don't like—then cultivate it. That's the part of your work that's individual and worth keeping.

Jean Cocteau

The important thing is that you make sure that neither the favorable nor the unfavorable critics move into your head and take part in the composition of your next work.

Thornton Wilder

I would recommend the cultivation of extreme indifference to both praise and blame because praise will lead you to vanity, and blame will lead you to self-pity, and both are bad for writers.

John Berryman

Criticism can never instruct or benefit you. Its chief effect is that of a telegram with dubious news. Praise leaves no glow behind, for it is a writer's habit to remember nothing good of himself. I have usually forgotten those who have admired my work, and seldom anyone who disliked it. Obviously, this is because praise is never enough and censure always too much.

Ben Hecht

Reading reviews of your own book is . . . a no-win game. If the review is flattering, one tends to feel vain and uneasy. If it is bad, one tends to feel exposed, found out. Neither feeling does you any good.

Walker Percy

The artists who want to be writers, read the reviews; the artists who want to write, don't.

William Faulkner

If upon reading the notices in the newspapers after the first night it is found that different critics take exception to different scenes, you can safely predict a successful run.

If the critics unanimously take exception to one particular scene it is advisable to move that scene to a more conspicuous place in the programme.

If, on the other hand, no particular critic dislikes any particular scene and they all write praising the production, it either means that you have such a good show that they haven't the face to attack it, or such a bad show that they like it. In either case it will probably be a failure.

Noël Coward

It is advantageous to an author that his book should be attacked as well as praised. Fame is a shuttlecock. If it be struck at only one end of the room, it will soon fall to the ground. To keep it up, it must be struck at both ends.

Samuel Johnson

I NEVER FOUND out the moon didn't come up in the west until I was a writer and Herschel Brickell, the literary critic, told me after I misplaced it in a story. He said valuable words to me about my new profession: "Always be sure you get your moon in the right part of the sky."

Eudora Welty

Never demean yourself by talking back to a critic. . . . Write those letters to the editor in your head, but don't put them on paper.

Truman Capote

Responding to criticism is a foolish thing for a writer to do, and an unpleasant one. It is much better to read only the advertisements of your work and note, briefly, your royalty reports. These will tell you how popular you are. How good you are, or are not, is a thing you should know only too well yourself.

Ben Hecht

The best thing you can do about critics is never say a word. In the end you have the last say, and they know it.

Tennessee Williams

The critics will always want to be the first to discover you and say how terrific you are. But then, when everyone else has discovered you, they want to be the first to say, "Well, you really are [expletive deleted] after all."

T. Coraghessan Boyle

Confronted by an absolutely infuriating review it is sometimes helpful for the victim to do a little personal research on the critic. Is there any truth to the rumor that he had no formal education beyond the age of eleven? In any event, is he able to construct a simple English sentence? Do his participles dangle? When moved to lyricism does he write "I had a fun time"? Was he ever arrested for burglary? I don't know that you will prove anything this way, but it is perfectly harmless and quite soothing.

Jean Kerr

As soon
Seek roses in December—ice in June;
Hope constancy in wind, or corn in chaff;
Believe a woman or an epitaph,
Or any other thing that's false, before
You trust in critics.

Lord Byron

It's a short walk from the hallelujah to the hoot.

Vladimir Nabokov

Dialogue

1. Dialogue should be brief.
2. It should add to the reader's present knowledge.
3. It should eliminate the routine exchanges of ordinary conversation.
4. It should convey a sense of spontaneity but eliminate the repetitiveness of real talk.
5. It should keep the story moving forward.
6. It should be revelatory of the speaker's character, both directly and indirectly.
7. It should show the relationships among people.

    Elizabeth Bowen

Dialogue has to show not only something about the speaker that is its own revelation, but also maybe something about the speaker that he doesn't know but the other character does know.

    Eudora Welty

Dialogue in fiction should be reserved for the culminating moments and regarded as the spray into which the great wave of narrative breaks in curving toward the watcher on the shore.

    Edith Wharton

Good writers do not litter their sentences with adverbial garbage. They do not hold up signs reading "laughter!" or "applause!" The content of dialogue ought to suggest the mood.

James J. Kilpatrick

Nouns, verbs, are the workhorses of language. Especially in dialogue, don't say, "she said mincingly," or "he said boisterously." Just say, "he said, she said."

John P. Marquand

A man or woman who does not write good dialog is not a first-rate writer.

George V. Higgins

Dialogue that is written in dialect is very tiring to read. If you can do it brilliantly, fine. If other writers read your work and rave about your use of dialect, go for it. But be positive that you do it well, because otherwise it is a lot of work to read short stories or novels that are written in dialect. It makes our necks feel funny.

Anne Lamott

Dialogue which does not move the story along, or add to the mood of the story, or have an easily definable reason for being there at all (such as to establish important characterization), should be considered superfluous and therefore cut.

Bill Pronzini

To write successful dialogue the author must have access to the mind of all his characters, but the reader must not perceive any more than he would in real life.

William Sloane

Don't write stage directions. If it is not apparent what the character is trying to accomplish by saying the line, telling us *how* the character said it, or whether or not she moved to the couch isn't going to aid the case. We might understand better what the character *means,* but we aren't particularly going to *care.*

David Mamet

Remember that you should be able to identify each character by what he or she says. Each one must sound different from the others. And they should not all sound like you.

Anne Lamott

Discouragement

I think aspiring writers need as much *dis*couragement as we can muster. Nobody should undertake the life of a fiction writer—so unremunerative, so maddeningly beset by career vagaries—who has any other choice in the matter. Learn a trade! Flannery O'Connor said it best: "People are always asking me if the university stifles writers. I reply that it hasn't stifled enough of them. There's many a bestseller that could have been prevented by a good writing teacher."

I would recommend three books to make the scales fall from the starry eyes of literary aspirants. George Gissing's *New Grub Street* is a fictional portrait of the wages (generally lean) of the scribbling business in late Victorian England, but it is far from irrelevant to what goes on today on the Grubnet. Cyril Connolly's *Enemies of Promise* is a wittily mordant diagnosis of the many obstacles that stand between most writers and writing their masterpieces—the only reason, Connolly avers, that anyone should be writing at all. And Jay Martin's life of the snakebit genius Nathanael West offers perhaps the single worst case of futility in the annals of twentieth century American literature. Every flavor of ill fortune dogged West from start to (premature) finish. This is as bad as it gets.

If you can stare these three Gorgons in the eye and not turn to stone or apply to law school, you may have what it takes.

Gerald Howard

I would never encourage anyone to be a writer. It's too hard.

Eudora Welty

I really don't want to encourage younger writers. Keep them down and out and silent is my motto. Do they talk about encouraging younger actresses? No. You don't want any younger actress to come along and outshine you.

John Updike

In 1845, when Charlotte Brontë wrote the British poet Robert Southey asking if he thought she could be a successful writer, his reply was a "cooling admonition":

> *Literature cannot be the business of a woman's life, and it ought not to be. The more she is engaged in her proper duties, the less leisure she will have for it, even as an accomplishment and recreation. To those duties you have not yet been called, and when you are, you will be less eager for celebrity.*

She ignored the advice and, with her sisters Emily and Anne, produced a volume of poetry under male pseudonyms. And she published *Jane Eyre* the following year.

Writing is easy. All you do is sit down at a typewriter and open a vein.

Red Smith

Taking the question in general, I should say, in the case of many poets, that the most important thing for them to do . . . is to write as little as possible.

T. S. Eliot

The first thing a writer has to do is find another source of income. Then, after you have begged, borrowed, stolen, or saved up the money to give you time to write and you spend all of it staying alive while you write, and you write your heart out, after all that, maybe no one will publish it, and, if they publish it, maybe no one will read it.

Ellen Gilchrist

It is a tough racket. It can be pretty heartbreaking, and you really have to, deep down, have a toughness to yourself, or you're not going to be able to survive in the theater.

Edward Albee

....

Stick to Zen. Fuck the work.
Henry Miller,
IN A LETTER TO **Lawrence Durrell** (1989)

....

If you want to be remembered as a clever person and even as a benefactor of humanity, don't write a novel, or even talk about it; instead, compile tables of compound interest, assemble weather data running back seventy-five years, or develop in tabular form improved actuarial information. All more useful than anything "creative" most people could come up with, and less likely to subject the author to neglect, if not ridicule and contempt. In addition, it will be found that most people who seek attention and regard by announcing that they're writing a novel are actually so devoid of narrative talent that they can't hold the attention of a dinner table for thirty seconds, even with a dirty joke.

Paul Fussell

In 1935, after reading James Laughlin's poetry, Ezra Pound told him, "You're never going to be any good as a poet. Why don't you take up something useful?" The heir to the Jones & Laughlin Steel fortune took the advice and founded New Directions, which would go on to publish many of the twentieth century's most distinguished writers, including Pound, Tennessee Williams, Henry Miller, Dylan Thomas, William Carlos Williams, Delmore Schwartz, and Vladimir Nabokov. Laughlin kept writing poetry, too.

There's nobody out there waiting for it, and nobody's going to scold you if you don't do it.
Lynne Sharon Schwartz

It's easy, after all, not to be a writer. Most people aren't writers, and very little harm comes to them.
Julian Barnes

Advice to aspiring writers: Fasten your seat belts—it's going to be a bumpy ride.
Christopher Buckley

A writer's life is only ever acceptance or rejection, surfeit or famine, and nothing in between. That's an emotionally draining way to live. As a result, it isn't necessary to discourage young writers. Life will do that soon enough. There are yards of writers under the age of thirty, but not many who stay the course. The ones who do aren't necessarily the most gifted but those who can focus well, discipline themselves, persevere through hard times, and spring back after rejections that would cripple others.
Diane Ackerman

There is a scene in Stanley Ellin's first novel, *The Winter After This Summer*, in which a young guy being tossed out of college stops by to have a last drink with a favorite professor, and the older man says to the kid, "What are you going to do now? What do you want to be?" And the kid thinks about it for a moment and replies, "Well, I don't want to be a writer." And the professor toasts him, saying, "That's good. There are already too many people around who mistake a love of reading for a talent for writing." And that is my advice to young writers, too. Forget it. Take up plumbing or electrical wiring. The money is vastly better, and the work-hours are more reasonable, and when your toilet overflows, you don't want Dostoevski coming to your house.

So when I teach workshops, or lecture to "writers' groups," I do my best to discourage as many as possible. This is in no way an attempt to lessen the competition, because I truly, deeply believe that writers are not in competition with each other. What I write, Joyce Carol Oates can't write; what Ms. Oates writes, Donald Westlake can't write; and what Kafka did has already been done, all that Hemingway bullshit about "pulling against Chekhov and that all time fast gun heavyweight puncher Tolstoy" notwithstanding. (Hemingway meant, it is now generally accepted, not that one had to go mano-a-mano with any other writer, but that in the words of John Simon—"there is no point in saying less than your predecessors have said.")

In the burning core of what I believe to be true about the art and craft of writing, I know that one *cannot* discourage a *real* writer. Like von Kleist, "I write only because I cannot stop." And that is the way of it for a *real* writer, not for the fuzzyheaded dreamer or parvenu who think's it's an easy way to make fame and fortune. You can break a real writer's hands, and s/he will tap out the words with nose or toes. Anyone who *can* be discouraged, *should* be. They will be happier and more useful to the commonweal as great ballerinas, fine sculptors, sensitive jurists, accomplished historians, imaginative scientists.

Harlan Ellison

....

Literature will neither yield thee bread, nor a stomach to digest bread with; quit it in God's name.

Thomas Carlyle,

IN A LETTER TO **Ralph Waldo Emerson** (1835)

....

Advice to aspiring biographers: Don't do it.

James Atlas

If you haven't got an idea for one, forget it. If you haven't got an idea you want to express on paper, in words, forget it. If you prefer putting paint on canvas, or rolls on your pianola or in your oven, forget it. You're going to be with this novel for a long, long time, so you'd better have *thought* about it before you start writing it.

Evan Hunter

LIKE ALL OTHER artists, writers are not "made." Samuel Butler advised a young man "who wanted to write" that he was too late: Writers are born.

Taylor Caldwell

Advice to young writers: Find another profession to be young in.

Joe Queenan

You will never be satisfied with what you do.

Fay Weldon

Having been unpopular in high school is not just cause for book publication.

Fran Lebowitz

Drink

Boozing does not necessarily have to go hand in hand with being a writer, as seems to be the concept in America. I therefore solemnly declare to all young men trying to become writers that they do not actually have to become drunkards first.

James Jones

American writers drink when they are "blocked" and drunkenness—being a kind of substitute for art—makes the block worse.

Anthony Burgess

You know what Lawrence said: "The novel is the highest example of subtle interrelatedness that man has discovered." I agree! And just consider for one second what drinking does to "subtle interrelatedness." Forget "subtle"; "interrelatedness" is what makes novels work—without it, you have no narrative momentum; you have incoherent rambling. Drunks ramble; so do books by drunks.

John Irving

One of the disadvantages of wine is that it makes a man mistake words for thoughts.

Samuel Johnson

In order to write at a high level of competence you need a comprehensive vocabulary, a keen sense of overall structure, and an inner beat or cadence. Your senses must be razor-sharp. Alcohol blunts those senses even as it releases self-restraint. Therefore many writers feel they are getting down to the real story after a belt or two, little realizing they are damaging their ability to tell the real story.

Rita Mae Brown

A good writer must have more than vin rosé in his veins, use more than Chablis for ink.

Edward Abbey

A man's prose style is very responsive—even a glass of sherry shows in a sentence.

John Cheever

Drinking makes you loquacious, as we all know, and if what you've got for company is a piece of paper, then you're going to talk to it. Just try to enunciate, and try to make sense.

Madison Smartt Bell

No one, ever, wrote anything as well even after one drink as he would have done without it.

Ring Lardner

Write first, drink later. To write you must be warm, fed, loved and sober.

Patrick McGrath

Finish each day before you begin the next, and interpose a solid wall of sleep between the two. This you cannot do without temperance.

Ralph Waldo Emerson

Writers who use alcohol to shut themselves down at the end of the day risk hangover or worse; heavy drinking damages short-term memory—exactly the kind of memory you need to juggle words and sentences and evoke associations as you write.

Richard Rhodes

First you take a drink, then the drink takes a drink, then the drink takes you.

F. Scott Fitzgerald

Get stewed:
Books are a load of crap.

Philip Larkin

Editors and Editing

There are, it seems, two kinds of editors. The first kind cares mainly about himself, about how his editing performance reflects on him and getting ahead or getting stroked or getting to lunch, as the case may be. Such editors are not editors at all and ought to go to breakfast and stay there. A real editor, however, is a rare thing, and I've been lucky in working with a few. A real editor is focused totally on the writer's work and helping the writer realize a vision of the piece or the book he's set out to do. Editing requires a certain selflessness that is hard to find.

David Remnick

The editor is a specialist about reading. His specialty is what is sufficiently general and common between a possible readership and what the author has to say. The tool he works with is himself. If the author cannot reach him, he can't reach the editor's readership either.

William Sloane

Being a free-lancer means that you accept the fact that the editor is an absolute despot as far as acceptance/rejection is concerned, and that from his decision, there is no appeal.

Isaac Asimov

THE BEST ADVICE on writing I've ever received was probably something Ted Solotaroff told me years ago when he was my editor. Going over a manuscript line by line again and again he kept reminding me, "Remember, this is your book, not my book. You're the one who's going to have to live with it the rest of your life. I might publish 30 or 40 books this year, you're only going to publish one, and probably the only one you're going to publish in two or three years."

Russell Banks

The editors are always right. Don't argue with them.

Mark Skousen

Bow down before them. They know what they are doing.

Quentin Crisp

In whatever manner possible, convince them that they can't live without you. Also, be a Boy Scout: be clean, bright, timely, obedient, useful, and brave. Then write a great piece.

Susan Orlean

Listen, then make up your own mind.

Gay Talese

Listen and learn.

Peter Mayle

Listen and nod—then put it back in later.

Whitney Balliett

Don't let any of them mess you about.

Conor Cruise O'Brien

Some editors will "get" what you write; others won't. The key is to have patience to learn from the criticisms of the former, the strength to ignore the indifference of the latter, and the wisdom (and great luck) to know the difference between the two.

Bruce Feirstein

THE BEST ADVICE I've ever received was from my first editor, Paul C. Smith, as I began my column in July 1938: "For God's sake, kid, be entertaining. And remember, I have a short attention span."

Herb Caen

One should fight like the devil the temptation to think well of editors. They are all, without exception—at least some of the time—incompetent or crazy. By the nature of their profession they read too much, with the result that they grow jaded and cannot see new talent though it dances in front of their eyes. Like writers, they are under insupportable pressures: they have to choose books that will sell, or at least bring the publisher honor, so they become hypercritical, gun-shy, cynical. Often they are consciously or (more often) unconsciously guided by unspoken policies of the publishing house or magazine they work for.... It is useful, in short, for young writers always to think of editors as limited people, though if possible one should treat them politely.

John Gardner

On the whole, I have found editors friendly and pleasant, but unpredictable and occasionally embarrassing in their desperation. So seldom do they get what they think they want that they tend to become incoherent in their insistent repetition of their needs. A writer does well to listen to them, but not too often, and not for too long.

Jerome Weidman

Editors make mistakes. By actual count, 121 publishers said "No thanks" to *Zen and the Art of Motorcycle Maintenance.* Roger Tory Peterson's *Field Guide to the Birds* and *Lolita* were turned down too, again and again. *The Clan of the Cave Bear, The Spy Who Came in from the Cold, The Peter Principle, Watership Down, To Kill a Mockingbird*—rejected, every one.

Judith Appelbaum

Don't let editors edit the life out of your sentences!

Isaac Asimov

Try to make them tell you what they really want. Most often they recognize what they *don't* want, but have a much harder time explaining what it is you're supposed to give them. Make them tell!

Maureen Orth

My advice on dealing with editors is to say yes to all suggestions unless you want to say no, to ask in those cases if the point might be set aside until later, and to proceed thus until all suggestions have been addressed. At that point, the writer should feel free to insist on having his or her way on the points set aside.

Thomas Powers

Abstinence is an unattainable ideal. Deserving of honesty and honor are the rare few, conspirators of kindred soul, who are capable themselves of such. As for the rest, suffer and con them, but never abdicate or surrender to them; for such is the nature of the racket.

Nick Tosches

....

Always remember that strange editors are not interested in your personality, but only in your work. If you tell them that you are down with leprosy, or about to be hanged, it only harrows their feelings without helping them in the slightest to do their jobs. Thus they resent it. When you send manuscripts to editors you don't know, say nothing whatever. Simply put your name and address in the upper left hand corner of the first page, insert your stamped and addressed return envelope, and let it go at that.

H. L. Mencken,
IN A LETTER TO **John Fante** (1932)

....

A good many young writers make the mistake of enclosing a stamped, self-addressed envelope, big enough for the manuscript to come back in. That is too much of a temptation to the editor.

Ring Lardner

AN EDITOR once asked me, "Are you writing every day?" I had to tell him no. Since then I've written every day.

Nicholson Baker

People who have never published anything sometimes ask me if they should send a query letter to a magazine or a publisher before undertaking a work of writing. I suggest they might want to do some writing first, and they look at me anxiously and fade away. I always wonder what planet they live on. Why should a businessperson—and editors are businesspeople, not patrons or creative writing teachers—take a chance without evidence on an unknown writer? If it were your money, would you?

Richard Rhodes

Don't try to guess what sort of thing editors want to publish or what you think the country is in a mood to read. Editors and readers don't know what they want to read until they read it. Besides, they're always looking for something new.

William Zinsser

The young editor of today has been raised in an environment dominated by movies, television, and similar technologies whose impact is ephemeral. He or she may therefore be more favorably disposed toward books that offer the quick jolt rather than the delicious lingering immersion into a work of complexity and sublety, one that challenges the intellect and demands an investment of time.

Richard Curtis

THE BEST ADVICE on writing I've ever received was, "Rewrite it!" A lot of editors said that. They were all right. Writing is really rewriting—making the story better, clearer, truer.

Robert Lipsyte

How to handle an editor: grieve for him/her.

Max Frankel

A good editor is a collaborator. Don't treat them like a censor. But don't defer too much.

Ken Auletta

Do what they ask until the piece doesn't feel like it's yours anymore. Then pull out for the kill fee or use another name if you need the money.

Corby Kummer

In spite of their real opinion of editors as parasites and literary phonies, authors should be extra polite to them at all times, remembering that in that direction lie some of the most tasty lunches available in New York.

Paul Fussell

THE BEST ADVICE on writing was given to me by my first editor, Michael Korda, of Simon and Schuster, while writing my first book. "Finish your first draft and then we'll talk," he said. It took me a long time to realize how good the advice was. Even if you write it wrong, write and finish your first draft. Only then, when you have a flawed whole, do you know what you have to fix.

Dominick Dunne

Never discuss a book idea with an editor at the end of the day or when he or she is preparing for a sales conference.

Bill Adler

Never expect your editor to actually *read* the manuscript.

Howard Ogden

Always remember that if editors were so damned smart, they would know how to dress.

Dave Barry

How to Handle an Incompetent Copy Editor ⌒

To: Book Editor [of a newspaper which shall remain nameless]
From: Florence King
November 23, 1997

I've just read my Fannie Hurst review and I'm appalled and mortified by the mistakes you managed to insert in it.

There is no excuse for this. I gave you another chance after the mess you made of my review of the Alice Keppel biography, but now I've had it. I will never review for you again. Your department is full of careless idiots who ought to be in an institution learning how to make brooms.

To: Letters to the Editor of the newspaper (not published)
From: Florence King
November 25, 1997

Your Book department's sloppy editing of my last two reviews has made me look like an ignoramus, so I am writing in self-defense to set the record straight.

In my Nov. 23 review of Imitations of Life: Fannie Hurst's Gaslight Sonatas, *by Abe C. Ravitz, a word dropped from a sentence destroyed my whole point.*

My version read: "Why would a Jewish novelist make the abused woman a gentile and the abusive man a Jew . . . ?"

The published version reads: "Why would a Jewish novelist make the abused woman and the abusive man a Jew . . . ?"

This is an erroneous description of Back Street, *with a grammatical error thrown in for good measure. Whoever did it also changed my correct spelling of Margaret Sullavan's name to "Sullivan."*

In my Aug. 31 review of Mrs. Keppel and Her Daughter, *by Diana Souhami, my first mention of the subject's name read: "the Hon. Mrs. George Keppel." This is the proper way to refer to the wife of a younger son of an earl, but your Book department deleted the "Hon."*

I wrote "William III" but somebody changed it to "William of England." There have been four Williams but never a "William of Eng-

land." I was referring to the William of William and Mary, but when he is mentioned alone he needs his III.

I referred to the "couturier" Edward Molyneux, but somebody changed it to "courtier."

This is inexcusable. I always file my copy twice, an electronic version and a fax version so that the first can be checked against the second, but obviously no one bothered to do it.

Then there is the matter of scheduling. I have never missed a deadline in my life; I always file my copy a week or two early, but Books has twice made it seem that I was late.

Last year I reviewed Flora Fraser's Caroline of Brunswick, about the unhappy marriage of George IV. It was a May book; I filed on Mar. 31 but Books ran it July 28, sitting on it throughout the Charles-Diana divorce proceedings that were supposed to be its tie-in.

Also in 1996 I reviewed Sally Bedell Smith's biography of Pamela Churchill Harriman. I filed on Sept. 24 but Books did not publish until Nov. 17, by which time all the other major outlets had already run their Harriman reviews. Moreover, two of your in-house columnists wrote columns about the Harriman book while my filed review went unpublished. Your Book department was scooped by its own paper.

I've had it. I can't go on writing letters of apology to authors for other people's stupidity and carelessness. I'll never review for your newspaper again.

To: Book Editor
From: Florence King
November 25, 1997

I have received your note and the guilty party's letter of apology. It made a great impression on me, though not the one he intended.

As I read it I fashioned a picture of him as a member of the over-forgiven generation. I can hear him now; sweet-talking his mother, sweet-talking his teachers, sweet-talking his girlfriend, but this is one woman he's not going to sweet-talk. Tell him for me to take his cajolery and shove it.

I am now wondering how many other of your reviewers have had experiences like mine. As we both know, many writers don't care what happens to their copy as long as they get the check; others do care but are afraid to rock the boat. Every word I write is a piece of my heart, so from now on I'll do their caring for them.

I intend to read every review with an eagle eye and mark all errors of fact, spelling, punctuation, bad grammar, and general knowledge, as well as all suspicious examples of tempo and euphony gone awry, and send them to you. You are badly in need of a proofreader and now you have one—after the fact, perhaps, but a proofreader just the same. Starting this coming Sunday I will be permanently poised over your shoulder and ready to pounce.

Encouragement

If you want to write, you can. Fear stops most people from writing, not lack of talent, whatever that is. Who am I? What right have I to speak? Who will listen to me if I do? You're a human being, with a unique story to tell, and you have every right. If you speak with passion, many of us will listen. We need stories to live, all of us. We live by story. Yours enlarges the circle.

Richard Rhodes

I have been writing a long time and have learned some things, not only from my own long hard work, but from a writing class I had for three years. In this class were all kinds of people: prosperous and poor, stenographers, housewives, salesmen, cultivated people and little servant girls who had never been to high school, timid people and bold ones, slow and quick ones.

This is what I learned: that everybody is talented, original and has something important to say.

Brenda Ueland

Believe in your own identity and your own opinions. Proceed with confidence, generating it, if necessary, by pure willpower. Writing is an act of ego and you might as well admit it. Use its energy to keep yourself going.

William Zinsser

The first question for the young writer to ask himself is: "Have I things in my head which I need to set forth, or do I merely want to be a writer?" Another way of putting it is, "Do I want to write— or *to have written?*" The ambition to be known as a writer is not in it- self unworthy, but it requires a deliberate search for likely subjects and a strong effort of thought and will to turn them into copy.

For a born writer the effort is altogether different. It is merely to choose from an abundance of ideas those which he thinks he is fit to handle—fit, that is, by reason of study, experience, and liter- ary skill. This last element is getting scarcer, it would seem, so that readers have to get cleverer at guessing riddles. Hence practicing to write well and finally writing well will repay. Editors and publishers will seek you out, the public will be carried away with love and gratitude.

Jacques Barzun

A note: despair at the badness of the book; can't think how I ever could write such stuff—and with such excitement: that's yesterday: today I think it good again. A note, by way of advising other Virginias with other books that this is the way of the thing: up down up down—and Lord know the truth.

Virginia Woolf

THE BEST ADVICE on writing I ever received was: *Invent your confidence.* When you're trying something new, insecurity and stage fright come with the territory. Many wonderful writers (and other artists) have been plagued by insecurity throughout their professional lives. How could it be otherwise? By its nature, art involves risk. It's not easy, but sometimes one has to invent one's confidence.

My own best advice to young writers is: follow your curiosity and passion. What fascinates you will probably fascinate others. But, even if it doesn't, you will have devoted your life to what you love. An important corollary is that it's no use trying to write like someone else. Discover what's uniquely yours.

Diane Ackerman

Keep going. Writing is finally play, and there's no reason why you should get paid for playing. If you're a real writer, you'll write no matter what.

Irwin Shaw

Writing a book is like driving a car at night. You only see as far as your headlights go, but you can make the whole trip that way.

E. L. Doctorow

You have to assume that the act of writing is the most important of all. If you start worrying about people's feelings, then you get nowhere at all.

Norman Mailer

Leave the dishes unwashed and the demands on your time unanswered. Be ruthless and refuse to do what people ask of you.

Lynne Sharon Schwartz

Every human being has exactly the same amount of time, and yet consider the output of Robert Louis Stevenson, John Peabody Harrington, Isaac Asimov, Ray Bradbury, William Goldman, Neil Simon, Joyce Carol Oates, Agatha Christie, and John Gardner. How did they accomplish what they have? They weren't deflected from their priorities by activities of lesser importance. The work continues, even though everything else may have to give. They know that their greatest resource is themselves. Wasting time is wasting themselves. When people ask them, "Where do you find the time?" they wonder, "Where do you lose it?"

Kenneth Atchity

WHEN I WAS doing short magazine pieces and screenplays, I feared undertaking anything as formidable as a book. One day, while I was collaborating with novelist Jerome Weidman on a screenplay for a studio, Weidman advised me how to overcome my fear. "Think about writing one page, merely one page, every day. At the end of 365 days, the end of a year, you have 365 pages. And you know what you have? You have a full-length book."

Irving Wallace

Be persistent. Editors change; editorial tastes change; markets change. Too many beginning writers give up too easily.

John Jakes

There's no substitute for persistence. It took me four years of clerk and copy boy's work before I caught a break. Also, a vow of poverty helps.

Phil Mushnick

For a true writer each book should be a new beginning where he tries again for something that is beyond attainment. He should always try for something that has never been done or that others have tried and failed. Then sometimes, with great luck, he will succeed.

Ernest Hemingway

One of the few things I know about writing is this: Spend it all, shoot it, play it, lose it all, right away, every time. Do not hoard what seems good for a later place in the book, or for another book, give it, give it all, give it now.

Annie Dillard

Sometimes people say to me, "I want to write, but I have five kids, a full-time job, a wife who beats me, a tremendous debt to my parents," and so on.

I say to them, "There is no excuse. If you want to write, write. This is your life. You are responsible for it. You will not live forever. Don't wait. Make the time now, even if it is ten minutes once a week."

Natalie Goldberg

I have never understood why "hard work" is supposed to be pitiable. True, some work is soul destroying when it is done against the grain, but when it is part of "making," how can you grudge it? You get tired, of course, but the struggle, the challenge, the feeling of being extended as you never thought you could be is fulfilling and deeply, deeply satisfying.

Rumer Godden

Don't market yourself. Editors and readers don't know what they want until they see it. Scratch what itches. Write what you need to write, feed the hunger for meaning in your life. Play at the serious questions of life and death.

Donald M. Murray

Always dream and shoot higher than you know you can do. Don't bother just to be better than your contemporaries or predecessors. Try to be better than yourself.

William Faulkner

No one put a gun to your head and ordered you to become a writer. One writes out of his own choice and must be prepared to take the rough spots along the road with a certain equanimity, though allowed some grinding of the teeth.

Stanley Ellin

Nobody ever got started on a career as a writer by exercising good judgment, and no one ever will, either, so the sooner you break the habit of relying on yours, the faster you will advance. People with good judgment weigh the assurance of a comfortable living represented by the mariners' certificates that declare them masters of all ships, whether steam or sail, and masters of all oceans and all navigable rivers, and do not forsake such work in order to learn English and write books signed Joseph Conrad. People who have had hard lives but somehow found themselves fetched up in executive positions with prosperous West Coast oil firms do not drink and wench themselves out of such comfy billets in order in their middle age to write books as Raymond Chandler; that would be poor judgment. No one on the payroll of a New York newspaper would get drunk and chuck it all to become a free-lance writer, so there was no John O'Hara. When you have at last progressed to the junction that enforces the decision of whether to proceed further, by sending your stuff out, and refusing to remain a wistful urchin too afraid to beg, and you have sent the stuff, it is time to pause and rejoice.

George V. Higgins

Everything goes by the board: honor, pride, decency ... to get the book written. If a writer has to rob his mother, he will not hesitate; the "Ode on a Grecian Urn" is worth any number of old ladies.

William Faulkner

....

I don't preach patience to you, but cynicism; it is the most comforting of philosophies. You will get over your present difficulties only to run into something worse, and so on until the last sad scene. Make up your mind to it—and then make the best of it. That is, do the best you can within the limits of your chance. If you can't write a book a year, then write one every two years.

H. L. Mencken,

IN A LETTER TO HIS FUTURE WIFE,

Sara Powell Haardt

....

Be in love with yr life
Be crazy dumbsaint of the mind
Blow as deep as you want to blow
Write what you want bottomless from the bottom of the
    mind
Remove literary, grammatical and syntactical inhibition
Write in recollection and amazement for yourself
Jack Kerouac

Whatever you can do or dream you can, begin it;
Boldness has genius, power and magic in it.
Johann Wolfgang von Goethe

As a writer you are free. You are about the freest person that ever
was. Your freedom is what you have bought with your solitude.
Ursula K. Le Guin

Take out another notebook, pick up another pen, and just write,
just write, just write. In the middle of the world, make one positive
step. In the center of chaos, make one definitive act. Just write. Say
yes, stay alive, be awake. Just write. Just write. Just write.
Natalie Goldberg

To sum it all up, if you want to write, if you want to create, you
must be the most sublime fool that God ever turned out and sent
rambling.

You must write every single day of your life.

You must read dreadful dumb books and glorious books, and
let them wrestle in beautiful fights inside your head, vulgar one
moment, brilliant the next.

You must lurk in libraries and climb the stacks like ladders to sniff books like perfumes and wear books like hats upon your crazy heads.

I wish for you a wrestling match with your Creative Muse that will last a lifetime.

I wish craziness and foolishness and madness upon you.

May you live with hysteria, and out of it make fine stories— science fiction or otherwise.

Which finally means, may you be in love every day for the next 20,000 days. And out of that love, remake a world.

Ray Bradbury

Ever tried? Ever failed? No matter. Try again. Fail again. Fail better.

Samuel Beckett

Rejections don't *really* hurt after you stop bleeding, and even a rejection serves to introduce the writer's name to an editor, particularly if a rejected story is competently written.

Isaac Asimov

Just get it down on paper, and then we'll see what to do about it.

Maxwell Perkins

Type. Your job is to get it on paper. Ours is to decide if it's any good. Just keep typing.

Robert Gottlieb

The most solid advice ... for a writer is this, I think: Try to learn to breathe deeply, really to taste food when you eat, and when you sleep, really to sleep. Try as much as possible to be wholly alive, with all your might, and when you laugh, laugh like hell, and when you get angry, get good and angry. Try to be alive. You will be dead soon enough.

William Saroyan

It is never too late to be what you might have been.

George Eliot

Advice to Aspiring Writers ∽

From Jeffrey A. Carver's Web Page

Many people have e-mailed me asking what advice I might offer to an aspiring writer. Here are a few thoughts. A lot more could be said, obviously, but I hope you'll find the following useful:

• Read, read, read. Read widely and voraciously. Since you're looking at my web page, you probably have an interest in science fiction or fantasy (SF/F). Seek out the best in the field. (Look for my recommended reading list but only as a start; it doesn't even pretend to be exhaustive.) Read the classics, both SF and other. I wish I'd read more of the non-SF classics when I was in school.

• Practice, practice, practice writing. Writing is a craft that requires both talent and acquired skills. You learn by doing, by making mistakes and then seeing where you went wrong.

Short stories are a good training ground and an easier market to break into.

• If you're wondering about a course to pursue in college, and you think you want a career in writing, choose the school that you think will give you the best all-around experience. Much of what I learned in college I learned outside the classroom. Study what interests you (though it doesn't hurt to get some training for work that pays a salary!). What do you feel passionate about? Pursue it! You don't need a certificate to write; you do need self-discipline and inner fire.

• Write from the soul, not from some notion about what you think the marketplace wants. The market is fickle; the soul is eternal.

• Don't plan on making a lot of money from your writing. A survey by the Authors' Guild a few years ago found that the average author earned about $4,000 a year from his or her writing. That was a general survey, but even in the genres, there are plenty of people struggling—many of them quite good writers. If you make it into print, you are doing well. If you succeed in breaking out commercially, you will be among the fortunate few.

• Seek out constructive feedback on your work. Take suggestions seriously, and learn from them. Not all criticisms will be on the mark, but even those that aren't can help you spot problems that need attention. You must decide for yourself which suggestions to take, and which to leave. Writing workshops can be invaluable—not just to the aspiring writer but also to the working professional. I have belonged to a local writing group for over fifteen years, and they critique every piece of work I do before it goes to a publisher. My writing is far better for it. There are numerous online workshops available, both on the Internet and on the big commercial services. See my recommended reading list for a guidebook to writing workshops.

• Don't send me your manuscripts. I can't read them. I'm not an editor, and I'm busy trying to earn a living myself. Nor can I find you an agent or a publisher. You've got to do your own legwork. I know how hard it is, but there's just no other way.

• Seek out good sources of information. There are many fine books on writing, some of them general and some specifically oriented toward writing SF/F. The SFFWA (Science Fiction and Fantasy Writers of America) web page has links to numerous writer-friendly resources on the net. There's a link to the SFFWA page at the bottom of my home page. Your library has many resources as well. Ask to see *The Literary Marketplace*, which lists both publishers and agents.

• Be determined, and be thick-skinned. I collected rejection slips for six years before I finally sold my first short story.

Why did I keep going? Was I crazy? Probably. I was convinced I could do it, and I refused to take no for an answer.

• Once you decide you're ready to begin submitting to publishers, I suggest the following rule: Always have the next market in mind. If your story comes back with a rejection note, don't take it personally or stew about it. GET IT IN THE MAIL TO ANOTHER MARKET THAT SAME DAY. (Then you can go back to whatever it is you were doing, preferably writing the next story.)

Good luck, and I look forward to seeing your work in print!

Genres

Respect the genre you're writing in. In an effort to put your own stamp on it, don't ignore the established conventions of that genre—or you'll alienate your core audience of loyal buyers.

Kathleen Krull

[The] three characteristics a work of fiction must possess in order to be successful:

1. It must have a precise and suspenseful plot.
2. The author must feel a passionate urge to write it.
3. He must have the conviction, or at least the illusion, that he is the only one who can handle this particular theme.

Isaac Bashevis Singer

A short story must have a single mood and every sentence must build towards it.

Edgar Allan Poe

The short story makes a modest appeal for attention, slips up on your blind side and wrassles you to the mat before you know what's grabbed you.

Toni Cade Bambara

Don't put anything in a story that does not reveal character or advance the action.

Kurt Vonnegut

Reporting the extreme things as if they were the average things will start you on the art of fiction.

F. Scott Fitzgerald

Fiction is a lie, and good fiction is the truth inside the lie.

Stephen King

Good fiction is made of that which is real, and reality is difficult to come by.

Ralph Ellison

Good fiction is not preaching. If a writer is trying hard to convince you of something, then he or she should stick to nonfiction.

Terry McMillan

The problem with fiction, it has to be plausible. That's not true with non-fiction.

Tom Wolfe

The first thing you have to consider when writing a novel is your story, and then your story—and then your story!

Ford Madox Ford

One ought to know a lot about reality before one writes realistic novels.

Robert Stone

It is important that a novel be approached with some urgency. Spend too long on it, or have great gaps between writing sessions, and the unity of the work tends to be lost.

Anthony Burgess

Writing a novel is analogous to the theory of the expanding universe, the big bang, because the form stimulates widening out and out and out: You have firmament widening into firmament, you have all the space in the world. But a play is exactly the opposite, like a black hole: The fullness of the universe gets pulled back down into a single compact, dense atom and everything converges into that atom.

Cynthia Ozick

A novel has to limit itself to the crew of a ship or a family; it's not a great way to process a huge number of people.

Kurt Vonnegut

I think the key [in a political novel] is to establish the connection between political forces and individual lives. The questions to address are: How do social and political forces condition individual lives? How do the personal qualities of the players condition their political direction?

Robert Stone

What is a suspense novel? People in doubt, people mystified, people groping on their way from one situation to another, from childhood to middle age, from joy to sorrow—these are the figures in a true suspense novel. They are traveling along a road of uncertainty toward an unseen goal.

Daphne du Maurier

In any work that is truly creative, I believe, the writer cannot be omniscient in advance about the effects that he proposes to produce. The suspense of the novel is not only in the reader, but in the novelist, who is intensely curious about what will happen to the hero.

Mary McCarthy

I'VE JUST STARTED writing fiction, and I haven't really sought out advice on how to do it, but my friend Susanna Moore, the novelist, gave me a very good piece anyway. "Almost every novel," she told me, "is a mystery novel."

Kurt Andersen

A murder occurs; many are suspected; all but one suspect, who is the murderer, are eliminated; the murderer is arrested or dies.

W. H. Auden's FORMULA FOR A MYSTERY NOVEL

The mystery's very much the modern morality play. You have an almost ritual killing and a victim, you have a murderer who in some sense represents the forces of evil, you have your detective coming in—very likely to avenge the death—who represents justice, retribution. And in the end you restore order out of disorder.

P. D. James

Ten Commandments for the Detective Novel

1. It must be credibly motivated, both as to the original situation and the denouement.
2. It must be technically sound as to the methods of murder and detection.
3. It must be realistic in character, setting, and atmosphere. It must be about real people in a real world.
4. It must have a sound story value apart from the mystery ele-

ment; i.e., the investigation itself must be an adventure worth reading.

5. It must have enough essential simplicity to be explained easily when the time comes.
6. It must baffle a reasonably intelligent reader.
7. The solution must seem inevitable once revealed.
8. It must not try to do everything at once. If it is a puzzle story operating in a rather cool, reasonable atmosphere, it cannot also be a violent adventure or a passionate romance.
9. It must punish the criminal in one way or another, not necessarily by operation of the law.... If the detective fails to resolve the consequences of the crime, the story is an unresolved chord and leaves irritation behind it.
10. It must be honest with the reader.

   Raymond Chandler

The beginner who submits a detective novel longer than 80,000 words is courting rejection.

   Howard Haycraft

The detective himself should never turn out to be the culprit.

   S. S. Van Dine

How easily distracted the reader is—how much care you must take—depends on what you're writing. Judging from the evidence of best-sellers, readers of genre fiction are tolerant of what any writing teacher worth his salt would call sloppy writing, so long as the writer pushes the right genre buttons. If the spies intrigue, if the romance blossoms, if the horrors haunt, devoted readers apparently don't notice the quality of the writer's prose or don't care. I know of at least one popular, best-selling genre author who carefully goes through his draft manuscripts and substitutes clichés for any original turns of phrase that may have crept in, because he doesn't want to distract his readers with unfamiliar words and images and because he's established a consistent (clichéd) authorial voice across his shelf of books that he knows his readers expect to hear. Literary critics, who tend to judge all writing by the same high standard, may groan at these facts of life; genre readers read on enthusiastically, and genre writers laugh all the way to the bank.

Richard Rhodes

A good science fiction story usually deals with a society distinctly different from the one we are familiar with; a society that does not exist and has never existed; that is completely imaginary. That imaginary society has to be built up in detail without internal contradiction even while the plot is unfolding. The society can't be skimped; it should (at its best) be as interesting as the plot and catch just as strongly at the reader's attention.

Isaac Asimov

In science fiction, the characters are not always human beings. They can be alien creatures, robots, computers, or even intelligent dolphins. *But they must behave like humans,* or they will either bore or baffle the reader. Each character, no matter what he/she/it looks like, must experience human problems and show some semblance of human emotions. Think of Spock, on TV's classic *Star Trek* series. He is alien in appearance and most of the time he is alien in behavior. But underneath it all (and not so deep that the viewer cannot see it), Spock has human emotions of loyalty, courage, humor and love.

Ben Bova

Writing history...is similar to accounting: you enter facts into the accounting system you've devised and support each entry with a document delivered into the system from the real world. I was going to say writing history is more creative than that, but then we've all heard about how creative accounting can be.

Richard Rhodes

In writing biography, fact and fiction shouldn't be mixed. And if they are, the fiction parts should be printed in red ink, the fact parts in black ink.

Catherine Drinker Bowen

Editorial lesson: It is important for the sake of truth and history to have written the best biography of your subject; but it can be more lucrative to be first on the scene.

Peter Davison

I believe the secret of biography resides in finding the link between talent and achievement. A biography seems irrelevant if it doesn't discover the overlap between what the individual did and the life that made this possible. Without discovering that, you have shapeless happenings and gossip.

Leon Edel

In the biographies I most admire, the story moves forward implacably, inevitably. The reader *believes* in Mary Tudor, Elizabeth the Great, Lord Melbourne, George Sand (*Lélia*), Balzac (*Prometheus*). The reader cannot but believe. There are no awkward hurdles, no holes to fall through. Nothing is stretched too far or condensed to the point of collapse. The narrative—the plot—contains us, we know where we are going.

Catherine Drinker Bowen

Readers of biographies like their meat rare.

Robertson Davies

Should the autobiographer plan to begin his tale at the beginning? Usually not: the exit from the womb takes pretty much the same course for all of us and is of principal interest to obstetricians. If the autobiographer can settle on a later, essentially formative scene or episode, in childhood or adulthood, that somehow opens the door to the style and tilt for the whole book, the story stands a better chance of telling itself from start to finish in such a way as to cast the most revealing angle of light over its events.

Peter Davison

You have to take pains in a memoir not to hang on the reader's arm, like a drunk, and say, "And then I did this and it was so interesting."

Annie Dillard

Here's what you need to know before you agree to be a "co-author" for a celebrity or "expert":

1. Your "collaborator," no matter how famous, will have a lot less expertise than promised, and you will have to do a great deal of research for which you'll receive neither credit nor compensation.
2. Your collaborator will not understand what writing involves, or how long it takes, or that a second draft is not a final draft

(never show your collaborator a first draft) or that reading a chapter and making suggestions is not the same as writing it in the first place.

3. You and your collaborator will both believe that the work—and hence the money—has been unfairly divided.

4. In short, an amicable divorce is easier to pull off than a happy collaboration.

Nancy Hathaway

[The need for] precision in comedy writing is absolute. If you don't do it right, you don't trigger that laugh.

Andy Rooney

Study Andy Rooney. Watch everything he does. And don't do it. Be funny about things that matter. Your opinion of Velcro doesn't.

P. J. O'Rourke

Advice to aspiring humor writers: Listen.

Christopher Buckley

Revise a *lot*. You can usually make it funnier.

Dave Barry

Truth is funnier than most things you can make up.

Margo Kaufman

Advice on writing light verse: Get a good rhyming dictionary. Clement Wood's is the best. Learn the forms. Be metric-perfect; nobody likes doggerel. Read Dorothy Parker, the last great light verse writer. (Ogden Nash, a special taste, rarely scans.) Con the press/TV for good ideas. Boil it down to no more than eight lines;

this isn't the 19th Century. Make the last line a zinger—funny, in your face, whatever.

W. H. Von Dreele

Light verse is not to be taken too lightly by the writer.

Richard Armour

My advice to young journalists is: Be a nuisance. Annoy the hell out of the city desk. You might get away with it.

I. F. Stone

Never take no from a bureaucrat—and it's amazing how many bureaucrats are out there; work like a dog; don't be afraid to ask what might seem to be a dumb question; write it the way you feel it.

Ira Berkow

My advice to young journalists is to learn to *listen*. Far too many young writers don't understand that listening is a key skill in writing. Too many of them hear only their own voices and as a result they squander one of the most potent tools in connection with writing well.

Claude Lewis

My advice to young financial writers—though I've rarely followed it myself: be concise.

Andrew Tobias

The key to successful writing in finance and economics is storytelling. Tell stories and you'll never be accused of writing boring stuff about Wall Street or the dismal science.

Mark Skousen

Advice to young sportswriters: Read. And think. But as little as possible about sports.

Thomas Boswell

WHEN I WAS a young newspaperman, an old, gray-haired sportswriter named Harry Grayson said to me: "Always remember: When you free-load, bitch. You maintain dignity."

Ira Berkow

Well-meaning people are always going to tell you to "write what you know." That's nonsense. Do that and you'll starve. In this business [sports writing] you've got to write what they'll pay you to write.

Herb Graffis

Get a job writing about something other than sports first.

Michael Bamberger

Learn to write. Never mind the damn statistics. If you like statistics become a CPA.

Jim Murray

Don't return your expense account without SIGNING it. That delays the reimbursement process.

Phil Mushnick

Advice on writing about baseball: leave it all to me.

Roger Angell

A good magazine article doesn't need an introduction, so don't begin with the background of your subject, how you happened to get interested in it, why the reader should read it, or how you obtained the information for it. Begin your article with conflict that produces tension, often revealed by including a brief example or anecdote and problem that will be resolved at the end. It's a good rule to start as near the end as possible and then plunge your reader into the central tension. When you've involved your reader in this way, weave in background facts or information as you think the reader needs it to understand the purpose and point of your piece.

Donald M. Murray

A saleable article builds a bridge to the reader and touches him where he lives. The wider the identity, the better the article. Ask yourself who will want to read your article. If very few, find another idea.

Louise Boggess

You can organize a magazine article rudimentarily as a sandwich: two slices of experience or reporting or essay filled with a primer on the subject under discussion. I used that structure in desperation more than once and even got by with it. More sophisticated organization requires interweaving. The best way to do that is to let your narrative determine when you stop and fill in the basics. You find something in your research that you believe readers will recognize and use that to open the story. When you come to a point that's likely to be unfamiliar, you cut away long enough to explain the context, then cut back to narrative, and so on through the article.

Richard Rhodes

You must write for children in the same way you do for adults, only better.

Maxim Gorky

Children like to read about success, whether it's winning the hand of the best princess or prince, saving a life, helping people who need it, beating the other team in the game of the year, or discovering another universe.

Janet and Isaac Asimov

Anybody who shifts gears when he writes for children is likely to wind up stripping his gears.

E. B. White

"First do no harm," says the Hippocratic oath for physicians. If writers of children's books had to take an oath it might begin, "First tell the truth."

William Zinsser

The primary requisite for writing well about food is a good appetite.

A. J. Liebling

If you're interested in food, become a cook. If you're interested in writing, become a food writer.

Alan Richman

Advice on writing about wine: No flowery descriptions—just straightforward commentary. A wine is good, mediocre, or bad. Period.

James Villas

Some rules for writing a play:

1. The story of a play must be the story of what happens within the mind or heart of a man or woman. It cannot deal primarily with external events. The external events are only symbolic of what goes on within.

2. The story of a play must be a conflict, and specifically, a conflict between the forces of good and evil within a single person. The good and evil to be defined, of course, as the audience wants to see them.

3. The protagonist of a play must represent the forces of good and must win, or, if he has been evil, must yield to the forces of the good, and know himself defeated.

4. The protagonist of a play cannot be a perfect person. If he were, he could not improve, and he must come out at the end of the play a more admirable human being than he went in.

Maxwell Anderson

There really are no characters in plays; there are *relationships.* Where there are only characters and no relationships, we have an unsatisfactory play.

Arthur Miller

One begins with two people on a stage, and one of them had better say something pretty damn quick.

Moss Hart

The difference between writing for stage and for television is almost an optical one. Language on the stage has to be slightly larger than life because it is being heard in a much larger space. Plot counts for less on the television screen because one is seeing the characters at closer quarters than in the theatre. The shape and plot of a stage play count for more in consequence of the distance between the audience and the action. A theatre audience has a perspective on a play as a television audience does not. The audience in a theatre is an entity as a television audience is not. On television the playwright is conversing. In the theatre he is (even when conversing) addressing a meeting. The stage aspires to the condition of art as television seldom does (which is not to say that it shouldn't). The most that can be said for these plays in that respect is that occasionally they stray into literature.

Alan Bennett

Writing a screenplay must look easy, since everybody in America seems to have one in the works. It's not easy at all; it's comparable to constructing a cuckoo clock blindfolded . . . it's like composing an elephantine, one-hundred-twenty-page haiku.

Richard Rhodes

I believe it was the late Rosalind Russell who gave this wisdom to a young actor: "Do you know what makes a movie work? Moments. Give the audience half a dozen moments they can remember, and they'll leave the theater happy."

I think she was right. And if you're lucky enough to write a movie with half a dozen moments, make damn sure they belong to the star.

William Goldman

DON'T CHANGE Stevenson just for the fun of rewriting him. You can kill a classic with "improvements." A big, sprawling novel, say *Bleak House*, you have to pare down to a continuity that will hold an audience for ninety or a hundred minutes. But remember, *Jekyll and Hyde* already has a continuity. We don't have to waste time hammering out a story line. What you have to do is visualize it, think of every scene as the camera will see it and not as you—or Stevenson—would describe it in prose.

Hollywood Producer **B. P. Schulberg** to his young son, **Budd**, who went on to write the Academy Award–winning screenplay for *On the Waterfront*

In a novel the hero can lay ten girls and marry a virgin for the finish. In a movie that is not allowed. The villain can lay anybody he wants, have as much fun as he wants cheating and stealing, getting rich, and whipping the servants. But you have to shoot him in the end. When he falls with a bullet in the forehead it is advisable that he clutch at the Gobelin tapestry on the wall and bring it down over his head like a symbolic shroud. Also, covered by such a tapestry, the actor does not have to hold his breath while being photographed as a dead man.

Herman Mankiewicz

An *allegory* is a metaphorical narrative in which the surface story and characters are intended to be taken as symbols pointing to an underlying, more significant meaning. *Pilgrim's Progress* and *The Faerie Queen* are usually cited as outstanding examples of the category. The dangers inherent in allegory are (a) obscurity, which may prevent the reader from deriving any meaning at all from the story, (b) unskillful presentation, which may lead the reader to derive the wrong meaning, and (c) obviousness, which makes employment of the device unnecessary.

Theodore M. Bernstein

You can't really write a romance now, it has been ceded to the bargain-basement depths of literature.

Paul Monette

To write a good love letter, you ought to begin without knowing what you mean to say, and to finish without knowing what you have written.

Jean-Jacques Rousseau

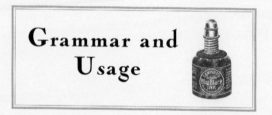

Grammar and Usage

You can be a little ungrammatical if you come from the right part of the country.

Robert Frost

Word has somehow got around that the split infinitive is always wrong. That is a piece with the outworn notion that it is always wrong to strike a lady.

James Thurber

It is indeed acceptable practice to sometimes split an infinitive. If infinitive-splitting makes available just the shade of meaning you desire or if avoiding the separation creates a confusing ambiguity or patent artificiality, you are entitled to happily go ahead and split!

Richard Lederer

USE SHORT SENTENCES. Use short first paragraphs. Use vigorous English. Be positive, not negative.

Eliminate every superfluous word.

Avoid the use of adjectives, especially such extravagant ones as splendid, gorgeous, grand, magnificent, etc.

Kansas City Star, EXCERPTS FROM THE STYLE SHEET,
WHICH, ACCORDING TO **Ernest Hemingway**,
WERE THE BEST WRITING RULES HE EVER LEARNED

When you catch an adjective, kill it.

Mark Twain

The adjective is the banana peel of the parts of speech.

Clifton Fadiman

The adjective is the enemy of the noun.

Voltaire

If the noun is good and the verb is strong, you almost never need an adjective.

J. Anthony Lukas

Don't say it was "delightful"; make *us* say "delightful" when we've read the description. You see, all those words (horrifying, wonderful, hideous, exquisite) are only like saying to your readers "Please will you do my job for me?"

C. S. Lewis

Forward motion in any piece of writing is carried by verbs. Verbs are the action words of the language and the most important. Turn to any passage on any page of a successful novel and notice the high percentage of verbs. Beginning writers always use too many adjectives and adverbs and generally use too many dependent clauses. Count your words and words of verbal force (like that word "force" I just used).

William Sloane

The editorial "we" has often been fatal to rising genius; though all the world knows that it is only a form of speech, very often employed by a single needy blockhead.

Thomas Babington Macaulay

Only presidents, editors and people with tapeworm have the right to use the editorial "we."

Mark Twain

It is almost impossible to write anything decent using the editorial "we," unless you are the Dionne family.

E. B. White

Our language contains perhaps a score of words that may be described as *absolute words.* These are words that properly admit of no comparison or intensification.... My own modest list of words that cannot be qualified by "very" or "rather" or "a little bit" includes *unique, imperative, universal, final, fatal, complete, virgin, pregnant, dead, equal, eternal, total, unanimous, essential,* and *indispensable.*

James J. Kilpatrick

1. Use contractions like *it's* or *doesn't.*
2. Leave out *that* whenever possible.
3. Use direct questions.
4. Use the pronouns *I, we, you,* and *they* as much as possible. Avoid using *it* and the passive voice.
5. If possible, put prepositions at the end.
6. When you refer back to a noun, repeat the noun or use a pronoun. Don't use "elegant variation."
7. Don't refer to what you *wrote* or are going to *write,* but to what

you *talked about* or are *going to talk about.* Don't use such words as *above, below,* or *hereafter;* instead, say *earlier, later, from now on.*

Rudolf Flesch's 7 *Ground Rules*

FOR HOW TO WRITE AS YOU TALK

Expressions such as "the former, the latter, the first, the second" should be used as seldom as possible: they are invitations to the reader's eye to travel back—and it should be encouraged always to read straight on at an even pace.

Robert Graves AND **Alan Hodge**

When "whom" is correct, recast the sentence.

William Safire

Avoid the passive voice whenever possible. University term papers bleed with the passive voice. It seems to be the accepted style of Academia. Dump it.

Rita Mae Brown

That. Which. That is the defining, or restrictive pronoun, *which* is the nondefining, or nonrestrictive. . . .

> *The lawn mower that is broken is in the garage. (Tells which one)*
> *The lawn mower, which is broken, is in the garage. (Adds a fact about the only lawn mower in question)*

The use of *which* for *that* is common in written and spoken language ("Let us now go even unto Bethlehem, and see this thing which is come to pass"). Occasionally *which* seems preferable to *that,* as in the sentence from the Bible. But it would be a convenience to all if these two pronouns were used with precision. The careful writer, watchful for small conveniences, goes *which*-hunting, removes the defining *whiches,* and by so doing improves his work.

William Strunk, Jr., AND **E. B. White**

Which normally refers to things, *who* to persons, and *that* to either persons or things.

Theodore M. Bernstein

Rule of thumb: If the qualifying phrase is set off by commas, use *which;* if not, use *that.*

James J. Kilpatrick

The great enemy of clear language is insincerity. When there is a gap between one's real and one's declared aims, one turns, as it were, instinctively to long words and exhausted idioms, like a cuttlefish squirting out ink.

George Orwell

Never use an abstract term if a concrete one will serve. Appeal directly to your reader's emotions rather than indirectly through the intermediary of the intellectualizing process. Tell him that the man *gave a dollar to the tramp* rather than that he *indulged in an act of generosity.*

David Lambuth

Never use a metaphor, simile or other figure of speech which you are used to seeing in print. Never use a long word where a short one will do. If it is possible to cut a word out, always cut it out. Never use the passive where you can use the active. Never use a foreign phrase, a scientific word or a jargon word if you can think of an everyday British equivalent. Break any of these rules sooner than say anything outright barbaric.

George Orwell

Use figures of speech sparingly. The simile is a common device and a useful one, but similes coming in rapid fire, one right on top of another, are more distracting than illuminating. The reader needs time to catch his breath; he can't be expected to compare everything with something else, and no relief in sight. When you use metaphor, do not mix it up. That is, don't start by calling something a swordfish and end by calling it an hourglass.

William Strunk, Jr., AND **E. B. White**

A simile must be as precise as a slide rule and as natural as the smell of dill.

Isaak Babel

Never use slang except in dialogue and then only when unavoidable. Because all slang goes sour in a short time.

Ernest Hemingway

Usage is the only test. I prefer a phrase that is easy and unaffected to a phrase that is grammatical.

W. Somerset Maugham

English usage is sometimes more than mere taste, judgment and education—sometimes it's sheer luck, like getting across a street.

E. B. White

THE BEST WRITING advice I've ever heard: Don't write like you went to college.

Alice Kahn

Avoid all prepositions and conjunctions that consist of more than one word. Aside from *inasmuch as*, this includes *with regard to, in association with, in connection with, with respect to, in the absence of, with a view to, in an effort to, in terms of, in order to, for the purpose of, for the reason that, in accordance with, in the neighborhood of, on the basis of*, and so on. There's not a single one of these word combinations that can't be replaced by a simple word like *if, for, to, by, about* or *since*.

Rudolf Flesch

Have no unreasonable fear of repetition. True, the repetition of a particular word several times in the same paragraph can strike a jarring note, but ordinarily the problem arises differently. The story is told of a feature writer who was doing a piece on the United Fruit Company. He spoke of bananas once; he spoke of bananas twice; he spoke of bananas yet a third time, and now he was desperate. "The world's leading shippers of the elongated yellow fruit," he wrote. A fourth banana would have been better.

James J. Kilpatrick

Prose alliteration should be used only for a special reason; when used by accident it falls upon the ear very disagreeably.

W. Somerset Maugham

How to Write Good ✑

Avoid run-on sentences that are hard to read.

No sentence fragments.

It behooves us to avoid archaisms.

Also, avoid awkward or affected alliteration.

Don't use no double negatives.

If I've told you once, I've told you a thousand times,
  "Resist hyperbole."

Avoid commas, that are not necessary.

Verbs has to agree with their subjects.

Avoid trendy locutions that sound flaky.

Writing carefully, dangling participles should not be used.

Kill all exclamation points!!!

Never use a long word when a diminutive one will do.

Proofread carefully to see if you any words out.

Take the bull by the hand and don't mix metaphors.

Don't verb nouns.

Never, ever use repetitive redundancies.

Last but not least, avoid clichés like the plague.

William Safire's "Fumblerules"
—MISTAKES THAT CALL ATTENTION
  TO THE RULE

Material

Find a subject you care about and which you in your heart feel others should care about. It is this genuine caring, not your games with language, which will be the most compelling and seductive element in your style.

Kurt Vonnegut

A writer looking for subjects inquires not after what he loves best, but after what he alone loves at all.

Annie Dillard

You can write about *anything*, and if you write well enough, even the reader with no intrinsic interest in the subject will become involved.

Tracy Kidder

You cannot write well without data.

George V. Higgins

THE BEST WRITING advice I've ever received is: "Facts are eloquent."

Norrie Epstein

Yvetot [a small town in the north of France] is as good as Constantinople.

Gustave Flaubert

If you have to urge a writing student to "gain experience with life," he is probably never going to be a writer. Any life will provide the material for writing, if it is attended to.

Wallace Stegner

Writers don't write from experience, though many are resistant to admit that they don't. I want to be clear about this. If you wrote from experience, you'd get maybe one book, maybe three poems. Writers write from empathy.

Nikki Giovanni

A novelist is stuck with his youth. We spend it without paying much attention to how it will work out as material; nevertheless, we must draw on whatever was there for the rest of our lives.

Vance Bourjaily

Every writer must articulate from the specific. They must reach down where they stand, because there is nothing else from which to draw.

Gloria Naylor

Very much of a novelist's work must appertain to the intercourse between young men and young women.

Anthony Trollope

Write about what you know personally, limited though it may be. Get your facts right. Try to write a story with a beginning, a middle and an end.

Frederick Forsyth

Study yr keeds. Kids. There are a lot of poems there. But don't write about yr kids. Write about the human, what's left of him, where he's going, what he dropped on the floor.

Charles Bukowski,

IN A LETTER TO **Ann Bauman** (1962)

One of the dumbest things you were ever taught was to write what you know. Because what you know is usually dull. Remember when you first wanted to be a writer? Eight or 10 years old, reading about thin-lipped heroes flying over mysterious viny jungles toward untold wonders? That's what you wanted to write about, about what you *didn't* know. So. What mysterious time and place *don't we know?*

Ken Kesey

Writing teachers invariably tell students, Write about what you know. That's, of course, what you have to do, but on the other hand, how do you know what you know until you've written it? Writing is knowing. What did Kafka know? The insurance business? So that kind of advice is foolish, because it presumes that you have to go out to a war to be able to do war. Well, some do and some don't. I've had very little experience in my life. In fact, I try to avoid experience if I can. Most experience is bad.

E. L. Doctorow

THE BEST ADVICE I've ever received was from Barbara Kafka: "Don't put in all you know—you will live to write again."

Corby Kummer

Writing fails because the writer does not know enough about his material. If he knows enough he will feel enough.

William Sloane

A poet ought not to pick nature's pocket: let him borrow, and so borrow as to repay by the very act of borrowing. Examine nature accurately, but write from recollection, and trust more to your imagination than to your memory.

Samuel Taylor Coleridge

Breathe in experience, breathe out poetry.

Muriel Rukeyser

Poke around.

William Carlos Williams

Write what makes you happy.

O. Henry

Write about what you're most afraid of.

Donald Barthelme

The effable is preferable to the ineffable.

Primo Levi

A writer should concern himself with whatever absorbs his fancy, stirs his heart, and unlimbers his typewriter.

E. B. White

Choice of subject is of cardinal importance. One does by far one's best work when besotted by and absorbed in the matter at hand.
Jessica Mitford

There are only two things to write about: life and death.
Edward Albee

Money

Write without pay until somebody offers pay; if nobody offers within three years, sawing wood is what you were intended for.

Mark Twain

Get all the money you can in front and cash the check quickly.

Larry L. King

Seek out the [editors] who have enough management clout to get you paid in full and on time and work only with them.

Andrew Cockburn

When trying to wrench money from a balky magazine that's held up your check for months, keep in mind that many of these periodicals are staffed by young girls with sizable trust funds. If you say, "I need the money to pay the rent," they will not be moved. However, if you call and say, "I don't want to cash in my T-Bill before it's due," they will issue a check immediately.

Margo Kaufman

BEST WRITING ADVICE I've ever received: Sell everything three times.

Margaret Carlson

The notion of making money by popular work, and then retiring to do good work on the proceeds, is the most familiar of all the devil's traps for artists.

Logan Pearsall Smith

The advance for a book should be at least as much as the cost of the lunch at which it was discussed.

Calvin Trillin

One great inhibition and obstacle to me was the thought: will it make money? But you find that if you are thinking of that all the time, either you don't make money because the work is so empty, dry, calculated and without life in it. Or you *do* make money and you are ashamed of your work.

Brenda Ueland

Write out of love; write out of instinct; write out of reason. But always for money.

Louis Untermeyer

Ignore the literary critics. Ignore the commercial hustlers. Disregard those best-selling paperbacks with embossed covers in the supermarkets and the supermarket bookstores. Waste no time applying for gifts and grants—when we want money from the rich we'll take it by force.

Edward Abbey

If you want to get rich from writing, write the sort of thing that's read by persons who move their lips when they're reading to themselves.

Don Marquis

There is no doubt about it, in the twentieth century if you are to come to be writing really writing you cannot make a living at it no not by writing.

Gertrude Stein

Your chances of making a living as a full-time writer are as good as your chances of playing first base for the New York Yankees.

Bill Adler

You must avoid giving hostages to fortune, like getting an expensive wife, an expensive house, and a style of living that never lets you afford the time to take the chance to write what you wish.

Irwin Shaw

Sir, no man but a blockhead ever wrote except for money.

Samuel Johnson

Occupational Hazards

The terror of the white page in the typewriter.

Tennessee Williams

One must avoid ambition in order to write. Otherwise something else is the goal: some kind of power beyond the power of language. And the power of language, it seems to me, is the only kind of power a writer is entitled to.

Cynthia Ozick

In Boston during the tryout of *The Odd Couple,* I had been up till four o'clock in the morning rewriting the third act—for the fifth time. Exhausted, I finally fell asleep on my typewriter. At seven A.M. a dentist from Salem, Mass., phoned to tell me how *he* would fix the third act. I thanked him and promised myself I would call him at five the next morning to tell him how I would fix his bridgework.

Neil Simon

It's nervous work. The state you need to write in is the state that others are paying large sums to get rid of.

Shirley Hazzard

The solitude of writing is ... quite frightening. It's close some-times to madness, one just disappears for a day and loses touch.

Nadine Gordimer

If you can lose a novel by talking it out, you can easily destroy a poem by not paying attention. I have lost many poems that way; I must lose one a week because I can't get to the typewriter or even to a piece of paper fast enough—sometimes I can't break through to silence, to solitude, to a closed door.

Marge Piercy

An author is a person who can never take innocent pleasure in vis-iting a bookstore again.

Say you go in and discover that there are no copies of your book on the shelves. You resent all the other books—I don't care if they are *Great Expectations, Life on the Mississippi* and the King James Bible—that are on the shelves. And then ... Say you are Ewell Loblate, author of *Don't Try This at Home.*

You go to the counter and ask, "Do you have that book, uh, *Don't,* uh, *Try This ... at Home?*" The clerk, who is listening to Black Sabbath through an earplug, looks blank.

"What's it on?" he says, after waiting to see whether you will leave.

"Oh, well, sort of ... autobiogra ... not *strictly,* but ..."

By now there is no doubt in the clerk's mind that even if you won't leave, you should.

"Who's the author?" he inquires.

"Uh, I believe ... something like ..." Oh, the horror! "Lollib ... Libl ... uh, Loblate?"

The clerk makes an indifferent noise. "I'll call downstairs."

"Oh, you needn't ..." But the machinery is in motion. After a long, long wait, as the clerk moves with understated sinuousness to some hellish cranial thrum and sells eleven copies of a book, on which high hopes are pinned, about weight loss through cats, here comes the conveyor belt, loudly, bearing a (the) copy of your book, blinking in the light.

Now, you don't want to *buy* your book. On an author's earnings, you can't afford it. On the other hand, you don't want to thumb through your book under the gaze of this person, this link to the reading public, and then say no, no thanks, you don't believe it is exactly what you had in mind.

But what you want most of all not to do is let the clerk catch sight of your picture on the jacket.

Which he does. "Hey!" he shouts, at last interested. "This looks like you!" More loudly. "This *you?*"

"Well . . . no. That is, I . . ."

"Hey, this is you! Hey! Here's an author! Asking for his own book! Hey, wouldn't they give you any? HEY!"

And all the shoppers in the store gather round and are joined from the street by several people who have never been in a bookstore before, and they all marvel and hoot and cry "Author!" and poke each other ("Says it's autobiographical!" cries the clerk), roll their eyes, press in to check the picture against your face for themselves, howl, then scatter, shaking their heads in disbelief. This happens to some authors several times a day.

Roy Blount, Jr.

Stay away from MFA writing programs and writing workshops. A short workshop occasionally will do, but if you are too involved with writing programs, you stop writing for yourself and begin writing for the instructor.

Susan Isaacs

You don't want to get stuck listening to the pathetic book ideas of losers. So, when people discover that you are a writer, tell them you do pieces for mortuary magazines.

    Cathy Crimmins

....

Darling, this is the trap: BELIEVE YOU ARE GOOD WHEN THEY TELL YOU YOU ARE GOOD AND YOU ARE THEREBY DEAD, DEAD, DEAD. Dead forever. Art is a day by day game of living and dying and if you live a little more than you die you are going to continue to create some pretty fair stuff, but if you die a little more than you live, you know the answer.

    Charles Bukowski,
    IN A LETTER TO **Ann Bauman** (1962)

....

Whatever you do . . . avoid piles.

    T. S. Eliot

Plagiarism

When a thing has been said and well said, have no scruple; take it and copy it. Give references? Why should you? Either your readers know where you have taken the passage and the precaution is needless, or they do not know and you humiliate them.

Anatole France

Steal! And egad, serve your best thoughts as gypsies do stolen children, disfigure them and make 'em pass for their own.

Richard Brinsley Sheridan

Theft, the unacknowledged borrowing of style or substance or method, is bad; don't do it. Credit your teachers.

Nicholson Baker

If you steal from one author it's plagiarism. If you steal from many, it's research.

Wilson Mizner

The best way to become a successful writer is to read good writing, remember it, and then forget where you remember it from.

Gene Fowler

Great literature must spring from an upheaval in the author's soul. If that upheaval is not present, then it must come from the works of any other author which happen to be handy and easily adapted.

Robert Benchley

Plagiarism can be easy, safe and rewarding if you follow one rule: Only plagiarize your own stuff. Not only is it not a criminal offense, it's extremely satisfying, since every writer believes deep in his heart that the finest words ever written, the only ones worth restating, are his own.

Alan Richman

There is no Sixth Commandment in art. The poet is entitled to lay his hands on whatever material he finds necessary for his work.

Heinrich Heine

Immature artists imitate. Mature artists steal.

Lionel Trilling

Plot

Plot grows out of character. If you focus on who the people in your story are, if you sit and write about two people you know and are getting to know better day by day, something is bound to happen.

Anne Lamott

I plot as I go. Many novelists write an outline that has almost as many pages as their ultimate book. Others knock out a brief synopsis.... Do what is comfortable. If you have to plot out every move your characters make, so be it. Just make sure there is a plausible purpose behind their machinations. A good reader can smell a phony plot a block away.

Clive Cussler

Any fiction should be a story. In any story there are three elements: persons, a situation, and the fact that in the end something has changed. If nothing has changed, it isn't a story.

Malcolm Cowley

In nearly all good fiction, the basic—all but inescapable—plot form is: A central character wants something, goes after it despite opposition (perhaps including his own doubts), and so arrives at a win, lose, or draw.

John Gardner

The story of a play must be a conflict, and specifically, a conflict between the forces of good and evil within a single person. The good and evil to be defined, of course, as the audience wants to see them.

Maxwell Anderson

Sequential causality is generally considered to be very important in plotting. It is often thought to be the difference between a simple story, which just presents events as arranged in their time sequence, and a true plot, in which one scene prepares for and leads into and *causes* the scene that comes after it.

Rust Hills

I like to think of what happens to characters in good novels and stories as knots—things keep knotting up. And by the end of the story—readers see an "unknotting" of sorts. Not what they expect, not the easy answers you get on TV, not wash and wear philosophies, but a reproduction of believable emotional experiences.

Terry McMillan

Let us define a plot. We have defined a story as a narrative of events arranged in their time-sequence. A plot is also a narrative of events, the emphasis falling on causality. "The king died and then the queen died," is a story. "The king died, and then the queen died of grief," is a plot.

E. M. Forster

E. M. Forster's familiar example, "The King died, and then the Queen," is a simple accounting of two facts. It could be a journalistic note on history, and we would go on from there. However, while it is not a plot, it may suggest one to a writer with imagination and the freedom to indulge his talent, so that he might add: "The Queen was in perfect health only last week, and no doubt she would be alive today if the King's mind had not been poisoned against her by Iago."

Hallie Burnett

If, in the first chapter, you say there is a gun hanging on the wall, you should make quite sure that it is going to be used further on in the story.

Anton Chekhov

Prizes

Just in case you should ever want to get a National Book Award I think I can give you some advice. First you have to have at least three good friends among the judges and then you have to have strong nerves, a commodious bladder and a good supply of bourbon. . . . We drove to New York and I went to Parlor B, Mezzanine C at the Commodore where there were quite a lot of people penned in by velvet ropes. . . . Then Clifton Fadiman said he was going to give us a plaque and a thousand dollars but all he gave us was a plaque. Then they took this away from us. Then Fadiman gave us the plaque again and they took it away again. Then we pretended to autograph books . . . and Fadiman gave us the plaque again and took it away again. Then I went to the bathroom. Then we went down stairs where there were more people. It cost ten dollars to get in. Fadiman gave the plaque and a check to Red Warren. Then Red made a ten minute speech about the poem as structure and structure as the poem and sat down in a chair with a sign on it saying POETRY WINNER. Then Katherine [sic] Bowen made a speech but I didn't listen to this because I was afraid I would forget my own speech. Then I made a speech and sat down in a chair that said FICTION WINNER and Randall Jarrell, who had just washed his beard, made a long speech the gist of which was that Bennet [sic] Cerf is a shit, that South Pacific is shitty and that people who look at the sixty-four thousand dollar question are virtual cocksuckers. This went on for forty-four minutes and the Random House contingent coughed all the way through it. Then some screens were removed and there was one of those bars made of a trestle table covered with a bedsheet and a couple of hundred highball glasses each containing two ice-cubes and a teaspoon of whiskey. . . . Then we went to Toots Shor's where there was one of those buffets they had for movie previews. Smoked butt, baked beans and one old turkey. All the publishers got drunk and sang *Down by The Old Mill-stream.* Then we went back to the hotel where there were some friends drinking my bourbon. They did this until about two. Then early in the morning I went to the Dave Garroway studio which is really a store window on fifty-second street and outside there were about four hundred women milling around and holding up signs saying: *HELLO MAMA. DORIS. SEND MONEY. GLADYS. HELP. IDA.* I was asked to wait in a green room where there was a chimpanzee drinking coffee, a man with a long beard and a lady in Arab costume practicing a song. She said the song was in Arabic and that it was about how the little raindrops fill up the big well. Then she went up and sang her song and then they said it was time for me to go up but it took two strong men pushing and pulling to get me into the studio and everybody on the street shouted: *It's Gary Moore.* I sat down at a baize-covered table and quivered like a bowlfull of chicken fat for fifteen minutes and then I drove Mary home. Mary took the check away from me and Ben hung the plaque up in his clubhouse which is in the woods and is made of two packing crates so I may not be any richer but I sure am a hell of a lot more nervous.

John Cheever,

IN A LETTER TO **John Weaver** (1958)

The House of Morgan . . . was my first book and something of a fairy-tale experience. It received fine reviews (except for a couple of well-placed stinkers), then won the National Book Award. Winning the National Book Award for your first book, by the way, is an efficient way to lose your writer friends. People are cheered by your success—but only up to a point.

Ron Chernow

When Gore Vidal was informed he'd been chosen for membership in the American Academy of Arts and Letters he reportedly said, "Thanks, but I already belong to the Diners Club."

Process

Use your eyes and ears. Think. Read . . . read . . . and still read. And then, when you have found your idea, don't be afraid of it—or of your pen and paper; write it down as nearly as possible as you would express it in speech; swiftly, un-selfconsciously, without stopping to think about the form of it all. Revise it afterwards— but only afterwards. To stop and think about form in mid-career, while the idea is in motion, is like throwing out your clutch halfway up a hill and having to start in low again. You never get back to your old momentum.

David Lambuth

Don't think and then write it down. Think on paper.

Harry Kemelman

Once you've got some words looking back at you, you can take two or three—throw them away and look for others.

Bernard Malamud

THE BEST ADVICE on writing I've ever received is from Henry Miller's *On Writing:* You have to write a million words before you find your voice as a writer.

Patrick McGrath

Write freely and as rapidly as possible and throw the whole thing on paper. Never correct or rewrite until the whole thing is down. Rewrite in process is usually found to be an excuse for not going on.

John Steinbeck

When your Daemon is in charge, do not try to think consciously. Drift, wait and obey.

Rudyard Kipling

If you write, good ideas must come welling up into you so that you have something to write. If good ideas do not come at once, or for a long time, do not be troubled at all. Wait for them. Put down little ideas no matter how insignificant they are. But do not feel, any more, guilty about idleness and solitude.

Brenda Ueland

THE BEST ADVICE on writing I've ever received was given to me, like so much else, by Hubert Selby, Jr.: to learn and to know that writing is not an act of the self, except perhaps as exorcism; that, in writing what is worth being written, one serves, as vessel and voice, a power greater than vessel and voice.

Nick Tosches

You do not need to leave your room. Remain sitting at your table and listen. Do not even listen, simply wait, be quite still and solitary. The world will freely offer itself to you to be unmasked, it has no choice, it will roll in ecstasy at your feet.

Franz Kafka

You can't wait for inspiration. You have to go after it with a club.

Jack London

THE ONLY GOOD piece of advice that I ever read about playwriting was from John Van Druten, who said, "Don't outline everything, because it makes the writing of the play a chore."

Neil Simon

First drafts are for learning what your novel or story is about.

Bernard Malamud

The only true creative aspect of writing is the first draft. That's when it's coming straight from your head and your heart, a direct tapping of the unconscious. The rest is donkey work. It is, however, donkey work that must be done.

Evan Hunter

Put your notes away before you begin a draft. What you remember is probably what should be remembered; what you forget is probably what should be forgotten. No matter; you'll have a chance to go back to your notes after the draft is completed. What is important is to achieve a draft which allows the writing to flow.

Donald M. Murray

Read and revise, reread and revise, keep reading and revising until your text seems adequate to your thought.

Jacques Barzun

Revision is just as important as any other part of writing and must be done *con amore.*

Evelyn Waugh

It would be crazy to begin revising immediately after finishing the first draft, and counter to the way the mind likes to create. You're exhausted. You deserve a vacation. Go away from the project for at least a week.

Kenneth Atchity

The process of writing is a process of inner expansion and reduction. It's like an accordion: You open it and then you bring it back, hoping that additional sound—a new clarity—may come out. It's all for clarity.

Jerzy Kosinski

The best writing is rewriting.

E. B. White

In the writing process, the more a thing cooks, the better.

Doris Lessing

I might write four lines or I might write twenty. I subtract and I add until I really hit something I want to do. You don't always whittle down, sometimes you whittle up.

Grace Paley

Prose is like hair; it shines with combing.

Gustave Flaubert

Scything, I think, is the best thing to do when you complete a work of fiction.

John Cheever

....

Never did tell you my theory of writing. If it isn't spontaneous, right unto the very sound of the mind, it can only be crafty and revised, by which the paradox arises, we get what a man has hidden, i.e., his craft, instead of what we need, what a man has shown, i.e. blown *(like jazz musician or rose)—*

The requirements for prose & verse are the same, i.e. blow—*What a man most wishes to hide, revise, and un-say, is precisely what Literature is waiting and bleeding for—Every doctor knows, every Prophet knows the convulsion of truth.—Let the writer open his mouth & yap it like Shakespeare and get said what is only irrecoverably said once in time the way it comes, for time is of the essence—*

Jack Kerouac,

IN A LETTER TO **Malcolm Cowley** (1955)

....

Discipline is never a restraint. It's an aid. The first commandment of the romantic school is: "Don't worry about grammar, spelling, punctuation, vocabulary, plot or structure—just let it come." That's not writing; that's vomiting, and it leads to uncontrolled, unreadable prose. Remember: Easy writing makes hard reading, but hard writing makes easy reading.

Florence King

You run it through your mind until your tuning fork is still.

Martin Amis

The real writing process is simply sitting there and typing the same old lines over and over and over and over and sheet after sheet after sheet gets filled with the same shit.

William Gass

[Writing is] a bit like shitting . . . if it's coming in dribs and drabs or not coming at all, or being forced out, or if you're missing the rhythm, it's no pleasure at all.

Germaine Greer

Don't ever write a novel unless it hurts like a hot turd coming out.

Charles Bukowski

First, you get the idea. It may germinate for a long time or it just pops into your head. And then you work out a structure. And when you feel confident enough, you start to write. And you have to allow yourself the liberty of writing poorly. You have to get the bulk of it done, and then you start to refine it. You have to put down less than marvelous material just to keep going to whatever you think the end is going to be—which may be something else altogether by the time you get there.

Larry Gelbart

It's like making a movie: All sorts of accidental things will happen after you've set up the cameras. So you get lucky. Something will happen at the edge of the set and perhaps you start to go with that; you get some footage of that. You come into it accidentally. You set the story in motion, and as you're watching this thing begin, all these opportunities will show up.

Kurt Vonnegut

The unconscious mind takes the germ of an idea and develops it, but usually this happens only when a writer has tried hard, and logically, to develop it himself. After he has given it up for a few hours, getting nowhere, a great advancement of the plot will pop into his head. I have been waked up in the night sometimes by a plot advancement or a solution of a problem that I had not even been dreaming about.

Patricia Highsmith

You never have to change anything you got up in the middle of the night to write.

Saul Bellow

If you know what you are going to write when you're writing a poem, it's going to be average. Creating a poem is a continual process of re-creating your ignorance, in the sense of not knowing what's coming next. A lot of poets historically have described a kind of trance. It's not like a Vedic trance where your eyes cross, and you float. It's a process not of knowing, but of unknowing, of learning again. The next word or phrase that's written has to feel as if it's being written for the first time, that you are discovering the meaning of the word as you put it down. That's the ideal luck of writing a poem.

Derek Walcott

Freewriting is the easiest way to get words on paper and the best all-around practice in writing that I know. To do a freewriting exercise, simply force yourself to write without stopping for ten minutes. Sometimes you will produce good writing, but that's not the goal. Sometimes you will produce garbage, but that's not the goal either. You may stay on one topic, you may flip repeatedly from one to another: it doesn't matter. Sometimes you will produce a good record of your stream of consciousness, but often you can't keep up. Speed is not the goal, though sometimes the process revs you up. If you can't think of anything to write, write about how that feels or repeat over and over "I have nothing to write" or "Nonsense" or "No." If you get stuck in the middle of a sentence or thought, just repeat the last word or phrase till something comes along. The only point is to keep writing. Or rather, that's the first point. For there are lots of goals of freewriting, but they are best served if, while you are doing it, you accept this single, simple, mechanical goal of simply not stopping. When you produce an exciting piece of writing, it doesn't mean you did it better than the time before when you wrote one sentence over and over for ten minutes. Both times you freewrote perfectly. The goal of freewriting is in the process, not the product.

Peter Elbow

Publicity and Promotion

It is dangerous to let the public behind the scenes. They are easily disillusioned and then they are angry with you, for it was the illusion they loved; they do not understand that what interests you is the way in which you have created the illusion. Anthony Trollope ceased to be read for thirty years because he confessed that he wrote at regular hours and took care to get the best price he could for his work.

W. Somerset Maugham

Beware the highly publicized autograph session at bookstores. It is terribly embarrassing to sit behind a tall stack of your own books for two hours while customers sidestep your table, throwing sneaky or hostile glances, en route to selecting an armful of cookbooks, diet books, and how-to books written by total strangers.

Larry L. King

There's nothing that puts the audience to sleep faster than an author reading his nonfiction prose. Yes, she/he can illustrate her/his talk with a few well-chosen paragraphs, but if you read five pages, expect snores. Of course, we expect writers of fiction to read. We want to *hear* their voices *read* their voices, but they should not read endlessly.... And we generally find that the bigger the author, the more pleasant he or she is. It's the insecure ones that complain about the number of books in the store or that the bookstore failed to bring in a large enough audience.

Carla Cohen, CO-OWNER, **Politics & Prose Books**

I am convinced as a member of the reading public that bad [author] photographs are bad business. I have been put off reading books, which otherwise looked rather attractive, by the puss of the author printed on the back of the dust cover.

Raymond Chandler

If you ever write something, and it is reviewed, and the review includes a photo of you, and both the photo and the review are bad, you will find that the photo is more painful.

Diane Johnson

Be completely clear within yourself about the purpose of the publicity, tour, speech, signing, etc. If you still think it's worthwhile, give it your best shot, and quit as soon as politely possible.

Sallie Tisdale

To promote a book you are expected to get it up eight or ten times a day, sometimes in Philadelphia.

Roy Blount, Jr.

These days, publicity tours are very important. If you are asked to go on one, go. Not everyone is asked. I always feel honored when my publisher asks me to go on the road or appear on television chat shows. I've become very good at it. I know how to sell my book. If the conversation veers away to another topic, I have learned how to bring it back to the book. Nothing annoys me more than to hear writers in the various television green rooms around the country bitch and moan about how boring the book tours are, or how exhausting. Get into it. Have fun. Most of the people you meet are great. You're selling your books, and you're building your reputation. What's so bad about that?

Dominick Dunne

The only authors who complain more about book tours than the authors who go are the authors whose publishers don't send them, i.e., go and remember you want people to read your books. Even writers need to work now and then.

Scott Turow

A boy has to peddle his book.

Truman Capote

You want to sound as perky and enthusiastic as possible, on a book tour, so your listening audience won't suspect that you really, deep down inside, don't want to talk about your book ever ever ever again. You have come to hate your book. Back at the beginning, you kind of liked it, but now you think of it as a large repulsive insect that cheerful hosts keep hauling out and sticking in your face and asking you to pet.

Dave Barry

Should you find yourself facing all of America at 8:00 A.M. remember this: Not many people will recall what you say. They will recall how you look and how you act. (Don't wear all white. It glares.)

Rita Mae Brown

When on a TV or radio talk show, count yourself lucky if your name is pronounced properly and the host doesn't try to make a fool of you. If the host is a celebrity, don't expect your book to have been read, and be grateful if the host seems half as interested in you as in himself or herself. You will be seen or heard by many people, but most of them don't care about you and don't read anyway.

Janet and Isaac Asimov

The most intolerable people are provincial celebrities.

Anton Chekhov

---

1. Decide and practice in advance what you're going to say on the air, then say it no matter what questions you're asked. Make your answers entertaining, staying focused on the subject of your book.
2. In most cases the interviewers have not read your book, and don't much care what you say; be respectful of them and their audience but remember they're interested in selling their show, not your book: that's your job.
3. Mention the title of your book, but if you plug it too often it only sounds obnoxious.
4. Before you ask your publicist to get you on "Oprah" or "NewsHour," watch the show for a week and figure out ways an episode could be built around you and your book. And remember that, statistically speaking, almost no authors get on "Oprah."
5. Publicity opportunities are limitless, and a good publicist will help you mine them, but a publicity plan will be only as effective as you are.

6. Send your publicist flowers! They get a lot of rejection pitching books; be the author they'll want to do a little something extra for.

Russell Perreault,

PUBLICITY DIRECTOR, **Oxford University Press**

Though fame is a help in selling books, it is of small use in writing them.

Ben Hecht

It's much more important to write than to be written about.

Gabriel García Márquez

Writers should be read—but neither seen nor heard.

Daphne du Maurier

Celebrity, even the modest sort that comes to writers, is an unhelpful exercise in self-consciousness. Celebrity is a mask that eats into the face. As soon as one is aware of being "somebody," to be watched and listened to with extra interest, input ceases, and the performer goes blind and deaf in his overanimation. One can either see or be seen. Most of the best fiction is written out of early impressions, taken in before the writer became conscious of himself as a writer. The best seeing is done by the hunted and the hunter, the vulnerable and the hungry; the "successful" writer acquires a film over his eyes. His eyes get fat. Self-importance is a thickened, occluding form of self-consciousness. The binge, the fling, the trip—all attempt to shake the film and get back under the dining room table, with a child's beautifully clear eyes.

John Updike

Writers who get written about become self-conscious. They develop a regrettable habit of looking at themselves through the eyes of other people. They are no longer alone, they have an investment in critical praise, and they think they must protect it. This leads to a diffusion of effort. The writer watches himself as he works. He grows more subtle and he pays for it by loss of organic dash.

Raymond Chandler

Publishers and Publishing

The odds against an unknown author getting a manuscript published by simply sending it to a publishing house are astronomical.

Edwin McDowell

The rules seem to be these: if you have written a successful novel, everyone invites you to write short stories. If you have written some good short stories, everyone wants you to write a novel. But nobody wants anything until you have already proved yourself by being published somewhere else.

James Michener

Publishers don't nurse you; they buy and sell you.

P. D. James

It is not wise to solicit the opinions of publishers—they become proud if you do.

Gore Vidal

Advice on dealing with publishers: Express gratitude when appropriate.

Cynthia Ozick

Every time you think you've been screwed by publishers in every possible way, you meet one who has read the *Kama Sutra*.

Cathy Crimmins

So much bitterness exists between writers and publishers, you have to eliminate the distractions. You've got to keep focused.

John Irving

I don't think it's a good idea for writers to think too much about the publishing world. I sense in a good many books, even in books by the best writers, an anxiety about how it will do in the marketplace. You can feel it on the page, a sort of sweat of calculation.

Elizabeth Hardwick

Publishing is a very mysterious business. It is hard to predict what kind of sale or reception a book will have, and advertising seems to do very little good.

Thomas Wolfe

I think it is the most curious lack of judgment to publish before you are ready. If there are echoes of other people in your work, you're not ready. If anybody has to help you rewrite your story, you're not ready. A story should be a finished work before it is shown.

Katherine Anne Porter

With one exception, any publication opportunity you can seize is worth seizing; ever-widening ripples move out from even the smallest splash.

Something more like a self-contained plop is all you're likely to get, however, if you resort to a vanity press. Vanity publishing is not the same as either subsidy publishing or self-publishing, though the terms are often used as if they were synonymous. Subsidy publishing is best defined by its guaranteed audience; self-publishing is partly defined by its realistic efforts to find an appropriate audience; vanity publishing frequently involves no audience at all.

Judith Appelbaum

Burn proofs when read. You shall have the book on publication.

George Meredith,

IN A LETTER TO **Lady Ulrica Duncombe** (1902)

When editors buy from a proposal—which is most of the time—they presume that the manuscript has yet to be written, which is true most of the time. I believe, therefore, that it is better not to disabuse them of this notion.

Better, I believe, to remove the manuscript from the submission process altogether and to submit a proposal for your book *even if it is already written.* In addition to giving the editor less to turn down, you will probably want to rework the manuscript anyway based on the editorial feedback you have received from the proposal.

John Boswell

Be exceedingly careful in choosing your agent or your publisher. Don't send the book to anyone who charges a fee for reading it or publishing it. In the real world of publishing, people pay *you* for your work. . . . Choose a publisher who has previously published your sort of book. Don't shotgun it around blindly. If your novel espouses atheism, don't send it to a religious publisher.

Evan Hunter

Go to a big book store that has lots of poetry books. Look them over and see if you find any affinity groups that you like among the magazines and publishing groups, people you dig or who might dig your mind. Send them your stuff.

Allen Ginsberg

One of the great writer's myths is the one about papering the walls with rejection slips. There are stories of proposals and manuscripts that were rejected twenty-five or thirty times and went on to become published books and even, in rare case, bestsellers. But these stories are so exceptional that when they do happen they immediately become part of publishing lore.

Part of playing the publisher's game is knowing when you have lost. If you have been flatly rejected by ten well-chosen editors then you will almost certainly be turned down by the next hundred. It would be far better to spend your time rethinking your idea, reworking your proposal, or maybe even abandoning that particular idea and moving on to something else.

John Boswell

Today is the first of August. It is hot, steamy and wet. It is raining. I am tempted to write a poem. But I remember what it said on one rejection slip: After a heavy rainfall, poems titled "Rain" pour in from across the nation.

Sylvia Plath

Do not expect your publisher to advertise your book. Or furnish intelligible royalty statements. Or send the check on time. Or fix the typos in the first edition. Or spell your name right on the jacket.

Howard Ogden

Punctuation

When speaking aloud, you punctuate constantly—with body language. Your listener hears commas, dashes, question marks, exclamation points, quotation marks as you shout, whisper, pause, wave your arms, roll your eyes, wrinkle your brow.

In writing, punctuation plays the role of body language. It helps readers hear you the way you want to be heard. Careful use of those little marks emphasizes the sound of your distinctive voice and keeps the reader from becoming bored or confused. . . . [Punctuation] exists to serve *you*. Don't be bullied into serving *it*.

Russell Baker

A story can be wrecked by a faulty rhythm in a sentence—especially if it occurs toward the end—or a mistake in paragraphing, even punctuation.

Truman Capote

The word "I'll" should not be divided so that the "I" is on one line and "'ll" on the next. The reader's attention, after the breaking up of "I'll," can never be successfully recaptured.

James Thurber

I WAS TAKING a course with Lionel Trilling and wrote a paper for him with an opening sentence that contained a parenthesis. He returned the paper with a wounding reprimand: "Never, never begin an essay with a parenthesis in the first sentence." Ever since then, I've made a point of starting out with a parenthesis in the first sentence.

Cynthia Ozick

Cut out all those exclamation marks. An exclamation mark is like laughing at your own joke.

F. Scott Fitzgerald

Exclamation marks, also called "notes of admiration," should be sparingly used. Queen Victoria used so many of them in her letters that a sentence by her that ends with a mere full-stop seems hardly worth reading.

Robert Graves AND **Alan Hodge**

The author of the style-book of the Oxford University Press of New York (quoted in Perrin's *Writer's Guide*) says, "If you take hyphens seriously you will surely go mad." You should not take hyphens seriously.

Sir Ernest Gowers

A paragraph should concern only one phase of a narrative or argument. This phase may be large or small, but must be self-contained.

Robert Graves AND **Alan Hodge**

Short paragraphs put air around what you write and make it look inviting, whereas one long chunk of type can discourage the reader from even starting to read.

William Zinsser

The use of commas cannot be learned by rule. Not only does conventional practice vary from period to period, but good writers of the same period differ among themselves.... The correct use of the comma—if there is such a thing as "correct" use—can only be acquired by common sense, observation and taste.

Sir Ernest Gowers

There's not much to be said about the period except that most writers don't reach it soon enough.

William Zinsser

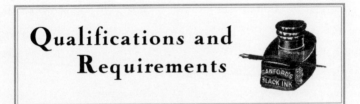

Qualifications and Requirements

I think that to write well and convincingly, one must be somewhat poisoned by emotion. Dislike, displeasure, resentment, fault-finding, imagination, passionate remonstrance, a sense of injustice—they all make fine fuel.

Edna Ferber

A novelist who would think himself of a superior essence to other men would miss the first condition of his calling. To have the gift of words is no such great matter. A man furnished with a long-range weapon does not become a hunter or a warrior by the mere possession of a firearm; many other qualities of character and temperament are necessary to make him either one or the other. Of him from whose armory of phrases one in a hundred thousand may perhaps hit the far-distant and elusive mark of art, I would ask that in his dealings with mankind he should be capable of giving a tender recognition to their obscure virtues. I would not have him impatient with their small failings and scornful of their errors. I would not have him expect too much gratitude from that humanity whose fate, as illustrated in individuals, it is open to him to depict as ridiculous or terrible. I would wish him to look with a large forgiveness at men's ideas and prejudices, which are by no means the outcome of malevolence, but depend on their education, their social status, even their professions.... I would wish him to enlarge his sympathies by patient and loving observation while he grows in mental power. It is in the impartial practice of life, if anywhere, that the promise of perfection for his art can be found rather than in the absurd formulas trying to prescribe this or that particular method of technique or conception. Let him mature the strength of his imagination among the things of this earth.

Joseph Conrad

Summon all your courage, exert all your vigilance, invoke all the gifts that Nature has been induced to bestow. Then let your rhythmical sense wind itself in and out among men and women, omnibuses, sparrows—whatever come along the street—until it has strung them together in one harmonious whole. That perhaps is your task—to find the relation between things that seem incompatible yet have a mysterious affinity, to absorb every experience that comes your way fearlessly and saturate it completely so that your poem is a whole, not a fragment; to re-think human life into poetry and so give us tragedy again and comedy by means of characters not spun out at length in the novelist's way, but condensed and synthesised in the poet's way—that is what we look to you to do now.

Virginia Woolf

I know everything. One has to, to write decently.

Henry James

An absolutely necessary part of a writer's equipment, almost as necessary as talent, is the ability to stand up under punishment, both the punishment the world hands out and the punishment he inflicts on himself.

Irwin Shaw

You have to have that feeling of "I'll show them." If you don't have it, don't become a writer. It's part of the animal, it's primitive, but if you don't want to rise above the crowd, forget it.

Leon Uris

An essential element for good writing is a good ear: One must listen to the sound of one's prose.

Barbara Tuchman

THE BEST ADVICE on writing I've ever received is to take it seriously, because to do it well is all-consuming.

David Guterson

Our tragedy today is a general and universal physical fear so long sustained by now that we can even bear it. There are no longer problems of the spirit. There is only the question: when will I be blown up? Because of this, the young man or woman writing today has forgotten the problems of the human heart in conflict with itself which alone can make good writing because only that is worth writing about, worth the agony and the sweat.

He must learn them again. He must teach himself that the basest of all things is to be afraid; and, teaching himself that, forget it forever, leaving no room in his workshop for anything but the old verities and truths of the heart, the old universal truths lacking which any story is ephemeral and doomed—love and honor and pity and pride and compassion and sacrifice. Until he does so, he labors under a curse. He writes not of love but of lust, of defeats in which nobody loses anything of value, of victories without hope and, worst of all, without pity or compassion. His griefs grieve on no universal bones, leaving no scars. He writes not of the heart but of the glands.

Until he relearns these things, he will write as though he stood among and watched the end of man. I decline to accept the end of man. It is easy enough to say that man is immortal simply because he will endure: that when the last ding-dong of doom has clanged and faded from the last worthless rock hanging tideless in the last red and dying evening, that even then there will still be one more sound: that of his puny inexhaustible voice, still talking. I refuse to accept this. I believe that man will not merely endure: he will prevail. He is immortal, not because he alone among creatures has an inexhaustible voice, but because he has a soul, a spirit capable of compassion and sacrifice and endurance. The poet's, the writer's, duty is to write about these things. It is his privilege to help man endure by lifting his heart, by reminding him of the courage and honor and hope and pride and compassion and pity and sacrifice which have been the glory of his past. The poet's voice need not merely be the record of man, it can be one of the props, the pillars to help him endure and prevail.

William Faulkner,
ACCEPTING THE **Nobel Prize for Literature,** 1950

To a chemist, nothing on earth is unclean. A writer must be as objective as a chemist; he must abandon the subjective line; he must know that dungheaps play a very respectable part in a landscape, and that evil passions are as inherent in life as good ones.

Anton Chekhov

The writer must be a psychologist, but a secret one; he must sense and know the roots of phenomena, but offer only the phenomena themselves as they blossom or wither.

Ivan Turgenev

Virginia Woolf said writers must be androgynous. I'll go a step further. You must be bisexual. If you can't carry out the act . . . that's up to you; you'd better get as close as you can imaginatively. You must create men who love women and women who love men or your books will be lopsided. In the beginning of everyone's work the dice are always loaded toward one's own sex or sex preference. Learning to unload those dice, to throw the bones honestly, is what maturity as an individual and as a writer is all about.

Rita Mae Brown

Although it is not necessary for a writer to be a prick, neither does it hurt. A writer is an eternal outsider, his nose pressed against whatever window on the other side of which he sees his material. Resentment sharpens his eye, hostility hones his killer instinct.

John Gregory Dunne

A first-rate college library with a comfortable campus around it is a fine milieu for a writer. There is, of course, the problem of educating the young.

Vladimir Nabokov

THEN IT WAS four o'clock, or nearly; it was time for Eliot to conclude our interview, and take tea with his colleagues. He stood up, slowly enough to give me time to stand upright before he did, granting me the face of knowing when to leave. When this tall, pale, dark-suited figure struggled successfully to its feet, and I had leapt to mine, we lingered a moment in the doorway, while I sputtered ponderous thanks, and he nodded smiling to acknowledge them. Then Eliot appeared to search for the right phrase with which to send me off. He looked at me in the eyes, and set off into a slow, meandering sentence. "Let me see," said T. S. Eliot, "forty years ago I went from Harvard to Oxford. Now you are going from Harvard to Oxford. What advice can I give you?" He paused delicately, shrewdly, while I waited with greed for the words which I would repeat for the rest of my life, the advice from elder to younger, setting me on the road of emulation. When he had ticked off the comedian's exact milliseconds of pause, he said, "Have you any long underwear?"

Donald Hall

A man of letters may have a mistress who makes books, but he must have a wife who makes shirts.

Denis Diderot

The writer's fundamental attempt is to understand the meaning of his own experiences. If he can't break through those issues that concern him deeply, he's not going to be very good.

Robert Penn Warren

The writer needs causal connection with his society, some sense that his work does something to make everyone's privacy a privilege rather than a burden.

Herbert Gold

Bad readers have asked me if I was drugged when I wrote some of my works. But that illustrates that they don't know anything about literature or drugs. To be a good writer you have to be absolutely lucid at every moment of writing, and in good health.

Gabriel García Márquez

A woman must have money and a room of her own if she is to write fiction.

Virginia Woolf

In order to paint you need equipment and a room and somebody to pay for the room. For a woman being a painter can be difficult. But all a writer needs is a pencil and a piece of paper and a corner and nobody noticing and the desire to do it; that's all it takes.

Fay Weldon

Appealing workplaces are to be avoided. One wants a room with no view, so imagination can meet memory in the dark.

Annie Dillard

What the writer needs is an empty day ahead.

Catherine Drinker Bowen

Rage is to writers what water is to fish.

Nikki Giovanni

The most essential gift for a good writer is a built-in shock-proof shit-detector.

Ernest Hemingway

A SUCCESSFUL LAWYER in Santa Fe decided he wanted to be a writer. He quit his job and the next Monday he began a novel, cold turkey, page one. He'd never written a word before that except for law briefs. He thought he could apply his lawyer's mind to his creative writing. He couldn't. Two years later, he was still struggling. I told him, "Bruce, you have to see the world differently, move through it differently. You've entered a different path. You can't just leap into the lake of writing in a three-piece suit. You need a different outfit to swim in."

Natalie Goldberg

A writer has to have some kind of compulsive drive to do his work. If you don't have it, you'd better find another kind of work, because it's only compulsion that will drive you through the psychological nightmares of writing.

John McPhee

A certain ruthlessness and a sense of alienation from society is as essential to creative writing as it is to armed robbery. The strong-armer isn't out merely to turn a fast buck any more than the poet is out solely to see his name on the cover of a book, whatever satisfaction that event may afford him. What both need most deeply is to get even.

Nelson Algren

If you want to be a novelist you have to know people. You have to know the dimensions in which they have lived, do live, or may live.

Morris L. West

I suppose that there are endeavors in which self-confidence is even more important than it is in writing—tightrope walking comes immediately to mind—but it's difficult for me to think of anybody producing much writing if his confidence is completely shot.

Calvin Trillin

The writer who loses his self-doubt, who gives way as he grows old to a sudden euphoria, to prolixity, should stop writing immediately: the time has come for him to lay aside his pen.

Colette

A writer needs three things, experience, observation and imagination, any two of which, at times any one of which, can supply the lack of the others.

William Faulkner

Real seriousness in regard to writing is one of two absolute necessities. The other, unfortunately, is talent.

Ernest Hemingway

I see the notion of talent as quite irrelevant. I see instead perseverance, application, industry, assiduity, will, will, will, desire, desire, desire.

Gordon Lish

If you have enough talent, you can get by after a fashion without guts, you can also get by, after a fashion again, without talent. But you certainly can't get by without either.

Raymond Chandler,
IN A LETTER TO **Carl Brandt** (1951)

You have to be a little patient if you're an artist: people don't always get you the first time.

Kate Millett

What is needed is, in the end, simply this: solitude, great inner solitude.

Rainer Maria Rilke

The Reader

No one can write decently who is distrustful of the reader's intelligence, or whose attitude is patronizing.

E. B. White

You must be aware that the reader is at least as bright as you are.

William Maxwell

We suggest that whenever anyone sits down to write he should imagine a crowd of his prospective readers (rather than a grammarian in cap and gown) looking over his shoulder. They will be asking such questions as: "What does this sentence mean?" "Why do you trouble to tell me that again?" "Why have you chosen such a ridiculous metaphor?" "Must I really read this long, limping sentence?" "Haven't you got your ideas muddled here?" By anticipating and listing as many of these questions as possible, the writer will discover certain tests of intelligibility to which he may regularly submit his work before he sends it off to the printer.

Robert Graves AND **Alan Hodge**

The writer is only free when he can tell the reader to go jump in the lake. You want, of course, to get what you have to show across to him, but whether he likes it or not is no concern of the writer.

Flannery O'Connor

If you despise your readers, they will probably despise you.

Andrew Greeley

A WRITER FRIEND advised, when I was starting out on my first book: "Write like you talk." I took that to mean that good writing must have a conversational quality, should not be arch or pretentious. And as you are aware when speaking to others when their attention lapses, so when writing you must think: How do I hold the reader's attention?

Ken Auletta

I write; let the reader learn to read.

Mark Harris

Keep in mind that the person to write for is yourself. Tell the story that you most desperately want to read.

Susan Isaacs

Better to write for yourself and have no public, than write for the public and have no self.

Cyril Connolly

If the stuff you're writing is not for yourself, it won't work.

Stephen King

An author who assures you that he writes for himself alone and that he does not care whether he is heard or not is a boaster and is deceiving either himself or you.

François Mauriac

There's no room for a reader in your mind: you don't think of anything but the language you're in.

E. L. Doctorow

Readers, after all, are making the world with you. You give them the materials, but it's the readers who build that world in their own minds.

Ursula K. Le Guin

It is the business of the writer to hide the fact that writing is his business. Readers are not interested in the mechanics of authorship.

A. A. Milne

The process of writing is something in which a writer's whole personality plays a part. A writer writes not only with his ideas but also with his instincts, with his intuition. The dark side of a personality also plays a very important role in the process of writing a book. The rational factor is something of which the writer is not totally aware. And so when a writer gives testimony about his books, he does it in a particularly subjective way. He gives a clear picture of only what he wanted to do, which rarely coincides with what he actually did. That is why a reader is sometimes in a better position to judge what a writer has done than the writer himself.

Mario Vargas Llosa

For the love of God don't condescend! Don't assume the attitude of saying, "See how clever I am, and what fun everybody else is!"

Charles Dickens,
IN A LETTER TO **Frank Stone** (1857)

Crass stupidities shall not be played upon the reader . . . by either the author or the people in the tale.

The personages of a tale shall confine themselves to possibilities and let miracles alone; or, if they venture a miracle, the author must so plausibly set it forth as to make it look possible and reasonable.

The author shall make the reader feel a deep interest in the personages of his tale and in their fate.

Mark Twain

There should be two main objects in ordinary prose writing: to convey a message, and to include in it nothing that will distract the reader's attention or check his habitual pace of reading—he should feel that he is seated at ease in a taxi, not riding a temperamental horse through traffic.

Robert Graves AND **Alan Hodge**

Never tell your reader what your story is about. Reading is a participatory sport. People do it because they are intelligent and enjoy figuring things out for themselves.

George V. Higgins

What lasts in the reader's mind is not the phrase but the effect the phrase created: laughter, tears, pain, joy. If the phrase is not affecting the reader, what's it *doing* there? Make it do its job or cut it without mercy or remorse.

Isaac Asimov

I want the reader to turn the page and keep on turning to the end. This is accomplished only when the narrative moves steadily ahead, not when it comes to a weary standstill, overloaded with every item uncovered in the research.

Barbara Tuchman

KURT VONNEGUT used to say to his class at Iowa, "You've got to be a good date for the reader."

John Casey

An author ought to write for the youth of his own generation, the critics of the next, and the schoolmasters of ever afterward.

F. Scott Fitzgerald

The author makes his readers, just as he makes his characters.

Henry James

The man who writes for fools is always sure of a large audience.

Arthur Schopenhauer

When you endeavor to be funny in every line you place an intolerable burden not only on yourself but on the reader. You have to allow the reader to breathe.

S. J. Perelman

A sentence may be as long as the writer pleases, provided that he confines it to a single connected range of ideas, and by careful punctuation prevents the reader from finding it either tedious or confusing.

Robert Graves AND **Alan Hodge**

The ordinary reader can only take in so many words in one gulp before his eyes come to a brief rest at a period. If the sentence has 30 words, he may have to pause for a moment and think. If it has over 40, chances are he's been unable to take in the full meaning.

Rudolf Flesch

A writer who questions the capacity of the person at the other end of the line is not a writer at all, merely a schemer.

E. B. White

Reading

Read, read, read. Read everything—trash, classics, good and bad, and see how they do it. Just like a carpenter who works as an apprentice and studies the master. Read! You'll absorb it. Then write. If it is good, you'll find out. If it's not, throw it out the window.

William Faulkner

Advice to aspiring poets: Poetry is not letter-writing cut up into lines. Become familiar with the poets that are the infrastructure of literature; read, read, read.

Cynthia Ozick

Read! Read! Read! And then read some more. When you find something that thrills you, take it apart paragraph by paragraph, line by line, word by word, to see what made it so wonderful. Then use those tricks the next time you write.

W. P. Kinsella

You can get what you need to write (as opposed to what you need to make a big nuisance of yourself at cocktail parties) by shutting yourself in a room by yourself for twenty minutes a day and reading aloud from E. B. White's *Charlotte's Web*, and going on from that to other works of skill, until you begin to see, *by hearing*, how much the choice and arrangement of the words contribute to the impact of the story, even when no sound is uttered in its reading. And you will begin to see, very quickly—guaranteed.

George V. Higgins

Examine what happens when you read. Young writers tend to forget or ignore what's actually going on when they're reading. Which is to say, when one reads, one has oral and visual hallucinations and it's the writer's job to control those oral and visual hallucinations. So I'm always trying to make young writers think about what goes on when they're sitting in a chair and reading fiction.

Russell Banks

Read as many of the great books as you can before the age of twenty-two.

James Michener

You have to saturate yourself with English poetry in order to compose English prose.

Vladimir Nabokov

When you start reading in a certain way, that's already the beginning of your writing. You're learning what you admire and you're learning to love other writers. The love of other writers is an important first step.

Tess Gallagher

"NEVER READ a book, Johnnie, and you will be a rich man."

Sir Timothy Shelley TO HIS SON, **Percy Bysshe Shelley,** WHO IGNORED THE ADVICE AND OFTEN READ SO AVIDLY THAT HE FORGOT TO EAT

If you are going to learn from other writers don't only read the great ones, because if you do that you'll get so filled with despair and the fear that you'll never be able to do anywhere near as well as they did that you'll stop writing. I recommend that you read a lot of bad stuff, too. It's very encouraging. "Hey, I can do so much better than this." Read the greatest stuff but read the stuff that isn't so great, too. Great stuff is very discouraging. If you read only Beckett and Chekhov, you'll go away and only deliver telegrams at Western Union.

Edward Albee

Read the best books first, or you may not have a chance to read them at all.

Henry David Thoreau

I REMEMBER [John] Gardner telling me, "Read all the Faulkner you can get your hands on, and then read all of Hemingway to clean the Faulkner out of your system."

Raymond Carver

If you read good books, when you write, good books will come out of you. Maybe it's not quite that easy, but if you want to learn something, go to the source. Basho, the great seventeenth-century Haiku master said, "If you want to know about a tree, go to the tree." If you want to know poetry, read it, listen to it. Let those patterns and forms be imprinted in you. Don't step away from poetry to analyze a poem with your logical mind. Enter poetry with your whole body. Dogen, a great Zen master, said, "If you walk in the mist, you get wet." So just listen, read, and write. Little by little, you will come closer to what you need to say and express it through your voice.

Natalie Goldberg

The greatest symbol of what writing is about is the full text version of the Oxford English Dictionary. The CD-ROM version is nice, but the physical enormity of the printed text gives a writer a sense of humility (if that is still possible), because the mountain to be scaled is the language. Auden used to sit on the first volume while at the dinner table, the better to stay even with language and with dinner. Any good teacher I've ever had—and the best was John McPhee—stressed the enormity of choice English provides, its capacity for clarity and ambiguity, dullness and thrill. It is the greatest invention ever devised (and re-devised). And, of course, the only way to get anywhere as a writer is to have read ceaselessly and then read some more. Pound (that rat) says somewhere that it is incredible to him that so many "poets" simply pick up a pen and start writing verse and call it poetry, while a would-be pianist knows full well how necessary it is to master scales and thousands of exercises before making music worthy of the name. Playing scales, for a writer, means reading. Is there any real writing that has no reading behind it? I don't think so.

David Remnick

WILLIAM SAFIRE told me something that really helped: "Never feel guilty about reading. That's what you *do.*"

Peggy Noonan

No one who intends to take up writing as a career should read any work that lies in the category in which his own efforts would be placed. If he disobeys this rule, he will almost certainly feel he must write literature instead of trying to say what he means.

Quentin Crisp

You can't write fiction unless you read fiction.

Bill Adler

If you are writing a manuscript so long that the prospect of not reading at all until you have finished is too intolerable, be sure to choose books which are as unlike your own book as possible: read technical books, history, or, best of all, books in other languages.

Dorothea Brande

Be sure that you go to the author to get at *his* meaning, not to find yours.

John Ruskin

Eschew the trashy and embrace the readworthy. Remember the acronym *GWIGWO:* Good Writing In, Good Writing Out.

William Safire

Rules and Commandments

I see but one rule: *to be clear.*

Stendhal

A good rule for writers: Do not explain overmuch.

W. Somerset Maugham

In a longish life as a professional writer, I have heard a thousand masterpieces talked out over bars, restaurant tables and love seats. I have never seen one of them in print. Books must be written, not talked.

Morris L. West

The author must keep his mouth shut when his work starts to speak.

Friedrich Wilhelm Nietzsche

If you require a practical rule of me, I will present you with this: Whenever you feel an impulse to perpetrate a piece of exceptionally fine writing, obey it—wholeheartedly—and delete it before sending your manuscript to press. Murder your darlings.

Arthur Quiller-Couch

The best rule for writing—as well as for speaking—is to use always the simplest words that will accurately convey your thought.

David Lambuth

There are simple maxims ... which I think might be commended to writers of expository prose. First: never use a long word if a short one will do. Second: if you want to make a statement with a great many qualifications, put some of the qualifications in separate sentences. Third: do not let the beginning of your sentence lead the readers to an expectation which is contradicted by the end.

Bertrand Russell

EITHER IT SOUNDS RIGHT OR IT DOESN'T SOUND RIGHT.

Isaac Asimov

The one great rule of composition is to speak the truth.

Henry David Thoreau

One of the great rules of art: do not linger.

André Gide

Don't get it right, get it written.

James Thurber

I have made three rules of writing for myself that are absolutes: Never take advice. Never show or discuss a work in progress. Never answer a critic.

Raymond Chandler

There are three rules for writing the novel. Unfortunately, no one knows what they are.

W. Somerset Maugham

Writing has laws of perspective, of light and shade, just as painting does, or music. If you are born knowing them, fine. If not, learn them. Then rearrange the rules to suit yourself.

Truman Capote

It's not wise to violate the rules until you know how to observe them.

T. S. Eliot

Beware of creating tedium! I know no guard against this so likely to be effective as the feeling of the writer himself. When once the sense that the thing is becoming long and has grown upon him, he may be sure that it will grow upon his readers.

Anthony Trollope

Keep it simple. Be clear. Think of your reader, not yourself. Cheer up.

Roger Angell

The idea is to write it so that people hear it and it slides through the brain and goes straight to the heart.

Maya Angelou

Never fear [the audience] or despise it. Coax it, charm it, interest it, stimulate it, shock it now and then if you must, make it laugh, make it cry, but above all...never, never, never bore the hell out of it.

Noël Coward

I WORKED IN the Hallmark public relations department for a man named Conrad Knickerbocker, the public relations manager, who had already begun publishing book reviews and fiction. After I got to know Knick a little, I asked him timidly how you become a writer.... He said, "Rhodes, you apply ass to chair." I call that solid gold advice the Knickerbocker Rule.

Richard Rhodes

Resist much, obey little.

Walt Whitman

Follow the accident, fear the fixed plan—that is the rule.

John Fowles

There are so many different kinds of writing and so many ways to work that the only rule is this: do what works. Almost everything has been tried and found to succeed for somebody. The methods, even the ideas, of successful writers contradict each other in a most heartening way, and the only element I find common to all successful writers is persistence—an overwhelming determination to succeed.

Sophy Burnham

The main rule of a writer is never to pity your manuscript. If you see something is no good, throw it away and begin again.

Isaac Bashevis Singer

There is probably some long-standing "rule" among writers, journalists, and other word-mongers that says: "When you start stealing from your own work you're in bad trouble." And it may be true.

Hunter S. Thompson

If I were to advise new writers, if I were to advise the new writer in myself, going into the theater of the Absurd, the almost-Absurd, the theater of Ideas, the any-kind-of-theater-at-all, I would advise like this:

> Tell me no pointless jokes.
> I will laugh at your refusal to allow me laughter.
> Build me no tension toward tears and refuse me my lamentations.
> I will go find me better wailing walls.
> Do not clench my fists for me and hide the target.
> I might strike you, instead.
> Above all, sicken me not unless you show me the way to the ship's rail.
>
> **Ray Bradbury**

Breslin's Rule: Don't trust a brilliant idea unless it survives the hangover.

Jimmy Breslin

Do not pay any attention to the rules other people make. . . . They make them for their own protection, and to hell with them.

William Saroyan

The Secret

The secret of good writing is to say an old thing in a new way or to say a new thing in an old way.

Richard Harding Davis

The first secret of good writing: We must look *intently*, and hear *intently*, and taste *intently*.

James J. Kilpatrick

The secret of all good writing is sound judgment.

Horace

Most people quit. If you don't quit, if you rewrite, if you keep publishing in fancier places, you will understand that "What's the secret?" is not *the question*, which is, "Are you having fun?"

Robert Lipsyte

The most important lesson in the writing trade is that any manuscript is improved if you cut away the fat.

Robert Heinlein

You have to surrender to the act of writing, give up to it, and trust that if you have anything, it will discover it for you.

E. L. Doctorow

I HEARD Joshua Logan interviewed on television. He told of a conversation he'd had with Maxwell Anderson about Anderson's successful plays. Was there some one thing, Logan asked him, that had served him above all else, one bit of advice he would give to young playwrights? Anderson advised that the main character must learn *something about himself* before the end of the play, and that this must be something that would *change his life forever.* Only then would an audience feel satisfied enough to make the play a success. Logan asked why there must be such satisfaction, and Anderson said, "... because otherwise they walk out of the theater."
> **Phyllis A. Whitney**

You have to throw yourself away when you write.
> **Maxwell Perkins**

Just get the right syllable in the proper place.
> **Jonathan Swift**

Rely on the sudden erection of your small dorsal hairs.
> **Vladimir Nabokov**

When you sit down to write, tell the truth from one moment to the next and see where it takes you.
> **David Mamet**

To young writers I give only two secrets that really exist ... all the other hints of Rosetta Stones are jiggery-pokery. The two secrets are these:

First, the most important book you can ever read, not only to prepare you as a writer, but to prepare you for life, is not the Bible or some handbook on syntax. It is the complete canon of Sherlock Holmes stories by Sir Arthur Conan Doyle.

The Holmes mysteries are nailed to the fixed point of logic and rational observation. They teach that ratiocination, and a denial of paralogia, go straight to the heart of Pasteur's admonition that "Chance favors the prepared mind." The more you know, the more unflinchingly you deny casual beliefs and Accepted Wisdom when it flies in the face of reality, the more carefully you observe the world and its people around you, the better chance you have of writing something meaningful and well-crafted.

From Doyle's stories an awakened intelligence can learn a *system* of rational behavior coupled with an ability to bring the process of deductive logic to bear on even the smallest measure of day-to-day existence. It works in life, and it works in art. We call it the writer's eye. And that, melded to talent and composure, is what one can find in the work of every fine writer.

The second secret, what they never tell you, is that yes, *anyone* can *become* a writer. Merely consider any novel by Judith Krantz and you'll know it's true. The trick is not to *become* a writer, it is to *stay* a writer. Day after day, year after year, book after book. And for that, you must keep working, even when it seems beyond you. In the words-to-live-by of Thomas Carlyle, "Produce! Produce! Were it but the pitifullest infinitesimal fraction of a Product, produce it in God's name! 'Tis the utmost thou has in thee: out with it, then. Up, up! Whatsoever thy hand findeth to do, do it with thy whole might. Work while it is called Today; for the Night cometh, wherein no man can work."

All that, and learn the accurate meaning of "viable," do not pronounce it *noo-kew-ler*, understand the difference between "in a moment" and "momentarily," and don't say "hopefully" when you mean "it is to be hoped" or "one hopes." Because, for one last quotation, as Molly Haskell has written: "language: the one tool that enables us to grasp hold of our lives and transcend our fate by understanding it."

Harlan Ellison

The only way to write is well and how you do it is your own damn business.

A. J. Liebling

Learn to write by doing it. Read widely and wisely. Increase your word power. Find your own individual voice through practicing constantly. Go through the world with your eyes and ears open and learn to express that experience in words.

P. D. James

One of the amusements of being old is that I have no illusions about my literary position. I have been taken very seriously, but I have also seen essays by clever young men on contemporary fiction who would never think of considering me. I no longer mind what people think. On the whole, I have done what I set out to do. Now my age makes everyone take me very seriously. If you are a writer, live a long time. I have found that longevity counts more than talent.

W. Somerset Maugham

Find what gave you emotion; what the action was that gave you excitement. Then write it down making it clear so that the reader can see it too. Prose is architecture, not interior decoration, and the Baroque is over.

Ernest Hemingway

Write what you really think and mean, not what you think you should think and not what you thought you would think and not what you hope it will mean, but what is really authentic and true.

Susan Orlean

The less one feels a thing, the more likely one is to express it as it really is.

Gustave Flaubert

No tears in the writer, no tears in the reader.

Robert Frost

Distance is essential. You stand on the outside and you look in.

John Edgar Wideman

THE BEST ADVICE on writing I've ever received: Miss Stein said, "The way to say it is to say it."

Quentin Crisp

Action is eloquence.

William Shakespeare

Make it new.

Ezra Pound

The shorter and the plainer the better.

Beatrix Potter

The secret of play-writing can be given in two maxims: stick to the point, and, whenever you can, cut.

W. Somerset Maugham

Every writer's assumption is that he is as other human beings are, and that they are more or less as he is. There's a principle of psychic unity. [Writing] was not meant to be an occult operation; it was not meant to be an esoteric secret.

Saul Bellow

THIRTY YEARS AGO my older brother, who was ten years old at the time, was trying to get a report on birds written that he'd had three months to write, which was due the next day. We were out at our family cabin in Bolinas, and he was at the kitchen table close to tears, surrounded by binder paper and pencils and unopened books on birds, immobilized by the hugeness of the task ahead. Then my father sat down beside him, put his arm around my brother's shoulder, and said, "Bird by bird, buddy. Just take it bird by bird."

Anne Lamott

Once the grammar has been learned, writing is simply talking on paper and in time learning what not to say.

Beryl Bainbridge

You don't write. You get out of the way.

Sallie Tisdale

The secret of good writing is telling the truth.

    Gordon Lish

There isn't any secret. You sit down and you start and that's it.

    Elmore Leonard

Style

You do not create a style. You work and develop yourself; your style is an emanation from your own being.

Katherine Anne Porter

Have something to say and say it as clearly as you can. That is the only secret of style.

Matthew Arnold

Be still when you have nothing to say; when genuine passion moves you, say what you've got to say, and say it hot.

D. H. Lawrence

Clear your mind of cant.

Samuel Johnson

THE BEST ADVICE on writing I've ever received is: "Write with *authority.*"

Cynthia Ozick

A good stylist should have narcissistic enjoyment as he works. He must be able to objectivize his work to such an extent that he catches himself feeling envious and has to jog his memory to find that he is himself the creator. In short, he must display that highest degree of objectivity which the world calls vanity.

Karl Kraus

You become a good writer just as you become a good joiner: by planing down your sentences.

Anatole France

THE BEST ADVICE on writing I've ever received was from Dwight Macdonald: "Everything about the same subject in the same place."

James Atlas

The greatest thing in style is to have command of metaphor.

Aristotle

Beware of the metaphor. It is the spirit of good prose. It gives the reader a picture, a glimpse of what the subject really looks like to the writer. But it is dangerous, can easily get tangled and insistent, and more so when it almost works: don't have a violent explosion pave the way for a new growth.

Sheridan Baker

Metaphor is supposed to state the unknown in terms of the known. It is supposed to say X equals Y. Yet when we say "John is a lion," we do not think of John with a mane, with four clawed paws, nor with a pompon-tipped tail. We extract from "lion" the emotional equivalent we need and let the rest go. The real metaphoric formula is X does-and-does-not-equal Y.

John Ciardi

The language must be careful and must appear effortless. It must not sweat. It must suggest and be provocative at the same time.

Toni Morrison

What is written without effort is in general read without pleasure.

Samuel Johnson

An author arrives at a good style when his language performs what is required of it without shyness.

Cyril Connolly

Ben Hecht received this advice from a newspaper editor: "When you write never get too fancy. Never put one foot on the mantelpiece, and be sure your style is so honest that you can put the word *shit* in any sentence without fear of consequence."

A good style comes primarily from lack of pretentiousness, and what is pretentious changes from year to year from day to day from minute to minute. We must be ever more careful. A man does not get old because he nears death; a man gets old because he can no longer see the false from the good.

Charles Bukowski

I don't know enough words to have a style; I know, at the most, fifteen adjectives.

Robert Benchley

Altogether, the style of a writer is a faithful representative of his mind; therefore, if any man wish to write a clear style, let him be first clear in his thoughts; and if any man would write in a noble style, let him first possess a noble soul.

Johann Wolfgang von Goethe

A good style must, first of all, be clear. It must not be mean or above the dignity of the subject. It must be appropriate.

Aristotle

Don't say you were a bit confused and sort of tired and a little depressed and somewhat annoyed. Be tired. Be confused. Be depressed. Be annoyed. Don't hedge your prose with little timidities. Good writing is lean and confident.

William Zinsser

Carefully examined, a good—an interesting—style will be found to consist in a constant succession of tiny, unobservable surprises.

Ford Madox Ford

A good style should show no sign of effort. What is written should seem a happy accident.

W. Somerset Maugham

A strict and succinct style is that, where you can take away nothing without loss, and that loss to be manifest.

Ben Jonson

The hardest thing about writing, in a sense, is not writing. I mean, the sentence is not intended to show you off, you know. It is not supposed to be "Look at me!" "Look, no hands!" It's supposed to be a pipeline between the reader and you. One condition of the sentence is to write so well that no one notices that you're writing.

James Baldwin

The greatest possible mint of style is to make the words absolutely disappear into the thought.

Nathaniel Hawthorne

When you say something, make sure you have said it. The chances of your having said it are only fair.

E. B. White

I am well aware that an addiction to silk underwear does not necessarily imply that one's feet are dirty. Nonetheless, style, like sheer silk, too often hides eczema.

Albert Camus

It was from Handel that I learned that style consists in force of assertion. If you can say a thing with one stroke, unanswerably you have style; if not, you are at best a *marchande de plaisir,* a decorative litterateur, or a musical confectioner, or a painter of fans with cupids and coquettes. Handel had power.

George Bernard Shaw

Nice writing isn't enough. It isn't enough to have smooth and pretty language. You have to surprise the reader frequently, you can't just be nice all the time. Provoke the reader. Astonish the reader. Writing that has no surprises is as bland as oatmeal. Surprise the reader with the unexpected verb or adjective. Use one startling adjective per page.

Anne Bernays

In all pointed sentences, some degree of accuracy must be sacrificed to conciseness.

Samuel Johnson

THE BEST ADVICE on writing I've ever received was from William Zinsser: "Be grateful for every word you can cut."

Christopher Buckley

A scrupulous writer, in every sentence that he writes, will ask himself at least four questions, thus: What am I trying to say? What words will express it? What image or idiom will make it clearer? Is this image fresh enough to have an effect? And he will probably ask himself two more: Could I put it more shortly? Have I said anything that is avoidably ugly?

George Orwell

Write with a smile, even when it's horrible or tragic.

Henry Miller

Always be a poet, even in prose.

Charles Pierre Baudelaire

Style is knowing who you are, what you want to say, and not giving a damn.

Gore Vidal

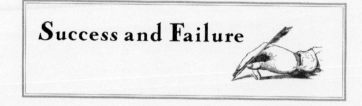

Success and Failure

You must once and for all give up being worried about successes and failures. Don't let that concern you. It's your duty to go on working steadily day by day, quite steadily, to be prepared for mistakes, which are inevitable, and for failures.

Anton Chekhov

As far as I can tell, the only healthy attitude for a writer is to consider praise, blame, book chat, and table position at Elaine's irrelevant to the writing, and to get on with it.

Jay McInerney

Success is feminine and like a woman; if you cringe before her she will override you. So the way to treat her is to show her the back of your hand. Then maybe she will do the crawling.

William Faulkner

Success makes you ridiculous; you end up wearing nightgowns to dinner.

Natalie Goldberg

Literary success of any enduring kind is made by refusing to do what publishers want, by refusing to write what the public wants, by refusing to accept any popular standard, by refusing to write anything to order.

Lafcadio Hearn

Make sure Rodgers and Hammerstein read your first book.

James Michener, WHOSE PULITZER PRIZE—WINNING
Tales of the South Pacific BECAME A LONG-RUNNING
BROADWAY MUSICAL, A BESTSELLER, AND A HIT MOVIE

It's terrible to have a success; everyone wants you to repeat it by writing the same thing over again.

Lawrence Durrell

Publication is not necessarily a sign of success.

William Sloane

The first book I wrote was the best-selling book of the year, and the second book dropped dead. What can we learn from this? Absolutely nothing. But if you keep on submitting and never give up, the chances are that someday somebody will eventually buy your work. Unless they don't.

Dan Greenburg

I never ask about sales. It's better not to know.

Alice Hoffman

I think what's most disturbing about success is that it's very hazardous to your health, as well as to your daily routine. Not only are there intrusions on your time, but there is a kind of corrosion of your own humility and sense of necessary workmanship. You get the idea that anything you do is in some way marvelous.

John Updike

Success and failure are both difficult to endure. Along with success come drugs, divorce, fornication, bullying, travel, meditation, medication, depression, neurosis and suicide. With failure comes failure.

Joseph Heller

Success and failure are equally disastrous.

Tennessee Williams

Technique

There is something in too much verbal felicity that can betray the writer into technique for the sake of technique.

Edward Abbey

Every novelist ought to invent his own technique.

François Mauriac

"I DO NOT THINK you can write a good short story without having a good story in you," Whit Burnett used to tell his class at Columbia University. "I would rather you had something to say with no technique, than have technique with nothing to say."

Hallie Burnett

The only principle of technique I'm aware of is faith. Faith to the language and faith to the situation to which that language points.

Charles Simic

The moment a man begins to talk about technique, that's proof he is fresh out of ideas.

Raymond Chandler

If technique is of no interest to a writer, I doubt that the writer is an artist.

Marianne Moore

The best technique is none at all.

Henry Miller

Be daring, take on anything. Don't labor over little cameo works in which every word is to be perfect. Technique holds a reader from sentence to sentence, but only content will stay in his mind.

Joyce Carol Oates

TOLSTOY TO RILKE, who was pestering him about techniques in writing: "If you want to write, write!"

Edward Abbey

When learning to play any instrument well, to wrestle, lift weights, dance, sing, write, it is wise to exercise. Try describing a hat in such a way the reader will realize its wearer has just had her dog run over. Practice putting your life into the present tense where you presumably lived it. Do dialogue—let's say—between a hobo and a high-class hooker, then between an ambulance chaser and a guy who sells scorecards at the ballpark—let's say—about the meaning of money. Between pints, get the arch of the dart down pat. Shoot foul shots day in and rim out. Pick a sentence at random from a randomly selected book, and another from another volume also chosen by chance; then write a paragraph which will be a reasonable bridge between them. And it does get easier to do what you have done, sing what you've so often sung; it gets so easy, sometimes, that what was once a challenge passes over into thoughtless routine. So the bar must be raised a few notches, one's handicap increased, the stakes trebled, tie both hands behind your back. Refuse the blindfold, refuse the final cigarette, refuse the proffered pizza. Do dialogue in dialect: a Welshman and a Scot arguing about an onion. Hardest of all: start over.

William H. Gass

Technique alone is never enough. You have to have passion. Technique alone is just an embroidered potholder.

Raymond Chandler

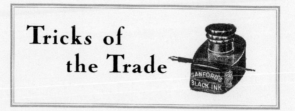

Tricks of
the Trade

In composing, as a general rule, run your pen through every other word you have written; you have no idea what vigor it will give to your style.

Sydney Smith

Read over your compositions and, when you meet a passage which you think is particularly fine, strike it out.

Samuel Johnson

FOR ADVICE on writing, nothing beats Nicolas Boileau, founder of the Académie Française, who wrote a creative-writing course in verse called *L'Art Poétique*. It dates to the mid-17th century but it's still the best around. The translation is by John Dryden. Some samples:

On cutting:

  Polish, repolish, every color lay,
  Sometimes add, but oftener take away.

On not messing up your murder mystery with a love story, and avoiding comic relief:

Remember always never to bring
A tame in union with a savage thing.

On avoiding too many subplots, unnecessary characters, and the
urge to put all you know in one book:

Make not your tale of accidents too full;
Too much variety will make it dull.
Achilles' rage alone, when wrought with skill,
Abundantly does a whole Iliad fill.

Florence King

I have found that a story leaves a deeper impression when it is impossible to tell which side the author is on.

Leo Tolstoy

When you depict sad or unlucky people, and want to touch the
reader's heart, try to be colder—it gives their grief, as it were, a
background, against which it stands out in greater relief. As it is,
your heroes weep and you sigh. Yes, you must be cold.

Anton Chekhov

Short stories can be rather stark and bare unless you put in the
right detail. . . . Details make stories human, and the more human a
story can be, the better.

V. S. Pritchett

Caress the detail, the divine detail.

Vladimir Nabokov

The correct detail is rarely exactly what happened; the most truthful detail is what *could* have happened, or what *should* have.

John Irving

A little inaccuracy sometimes saves tons of explanation.

Saki

THE BEST ADVICE on writing I've ever received is, "Knock 'em dead with that lead sentence."

Whitney Balliett

It is often necessary for a writer to distort the particulars of experience in order to see them better.

Wallace Stegner

Tell almost the whole story.

Anne Sexton

If you find a lot of explaining necessary, something is wrong with your material or with your approach to it.

James Gould Cozzens

You can't tell or show everything within the compass of a book. If you try to tell or show everything, your reader will die of boredom before the end of the first page. You must, therefore, ask yourself what is the core of the matter you wish to communicate to your reader? Having decided on the core of the matter, all that you tell him must relate to it and illustrate it more and more vividly.

Morris L. West

THE MOST USEFUL advice on writing I've ever received comes from Gil Rogin, who told me that he always uses his best thing in his lead, and his second best thing in his last paragraph; and from Dwight Macdonald, who wrote that the best advice he ever received was to put everything on the same subject in the same place. To these dictums I would add the advice to ask yourself repeatedly: what is this *about?*

Thomas Powers

Read what you've written aloud—you'll learn the rhythms that work for you.

Nat Hentoff

If you get the landscape right, the story will come from the landscape.

E. Annie Proulx

The more specific you are, the more universal you are.

Nancy Hale

Make the familiar exotic; the exotic familiar.

Bharati Mukherjee

I don't know anything about fingerprinting or ballistics or any of that stuff, and if you're any good you can fake most of that.

Robert B. Parker

Find out what your hero or heroine wants, and when he or she wakes up in the morning, just follow him or her all day.

Ray Bradbury

Begin with something interesting rather than beginning with something boring; begin with action rather than beginning with background information; speak about the characters after they have appeared rather than having them appear after having spoken about them.

Alexandre Dumas père

When the plot flags, bring in a man with a gun.

Raymond Chandler

Don't say the old lady screamed—bring her on and let her scream.

Mark Twain

The best playwrights—Tennesse Williams, for instance—will punctuate the most serious moment with an outrageous laugh. The audience delights in it. They need the relief. They need laughter. . . . The more an audience laughs, the more it feels. Shakespeare knew this—there's comedy in his most serious plays.

Jerome Lawrence

You have the right to not change anything, but don't be a fool. Change things if somebody else is right. But if you do change something because somebody else is right, you must instantly take credit for it yourself. That's very important.

Edward Albee

The trick is leaving out everything but the essential.

David Mamet

You can't clobber any reader while he's looking. You divert his attention, then you clobber him and he never knows what hit him.

Flannery O'Connor

Deliberately puzzling or confusing a reader may keep him reading for a while, but at too great an expense. Even just an "aura" of mystery in a story is usually just a lot of baloney. Who *are* these people? What are they up to? Provoking such questions from a reader can be a writer's way of deferring exposition until he feels the reader is ready for the explanation of it all. But more likely it's just fogging things up. A lot of beginning writers' fiction is like a lot of beginners' poetry: deliberately unintelligible so as to make the shallow seem deep.

Rust Hills

Life goes on, and for the sake of verisimilitude and realism, you cannot possibly give the impression of an ending: you must let something hang. A cheap interpretation of that would be to say that you must always leave a chance for a sequel. People die, love dies, but life does not die, and so long as people live, stories must have life at the end.

John O'Hara

HEMINGWAY GAVE a great piece of advice about writing, which I follow. He said always finish when you're in a little bit of a flow, for the next bout.

Edna O'Brien

Never write about a place until you're away from it, because it gives you perspective.

Ernest Hemingway

Sometimes you can lick an especially hard problem by facing it always the very first thing in the morning with the very freshest part of your mind. This has so often worked with me that I have an uncanny faith in it.

F. Scott Fitzgerald

One way of ending the poem is to turn it back on itself, like a serpent with its tail in its mouth.

Maxine Kumin

Don't tell anybody what your book is about and don't show it until it's finished. It's not that anybody will steal your idea but that all the energy that goes into the writing of your story will be dissipated.

David Wallechinsky

One of the oldest science fiction tricks . . . [is to] take an episode from history and "project" it onto the future. Isaac Asimov's brilliant *Foundation* trilogy began when Dr. Asimov began thinking about Gibbon's massive *The Decline and Fall of the Roman Empire.* My own first novel was a "projection" of the conquests of Alexander the Great into an interstellar setting.

Ben Bova

I sometimes suggest to inexperienced writers that they try to summarize their novels in progress in a sentence or two. It's a useful though limited way of finding out whether a book has a coherent theme, a theme that's likely to attract readers. "One day in the life of a humble prisoner in Stalin's gulag," or "one day in the life of a middle-aged mediocre Dublin Jew, explored as an odyssey," would convince most literate people that there was, at least, a worthy and intelligible subject.

D. M. Thomas

Make 'em laugh, make 'em wait, make 'em cry.

Wilkie Collins

Why You Write

Writing is like prostitution. First you do it for the love of it, then you do it for a few friends, and finally you do it for the money.

Molière

There are three reasons for becoming a writer: the first is that you need the money; the second, that you have something to say that you think the world should know; the third is that you can't think of what to do with the long winter evenings.

Quentin Crisp

You write because you want to be read.

William Styron

When you're writing, you're trying to find out something which you don't know.

James Baldwin

You don't write because you want to say something; you write because you've got something to say.

F. Scott Fitzgerald

You do not write a novel for praise, or thinking of your audience. You write for yourself; you work out between you and your pen the things that intrigue you.

Bret Easton Ellis

The only reason for being a professional writer is that you just can't help it.

Leo Rosten

Each of us is like a desert, and a literary work is like a cry from the desert, or like a pigeon let loose with a message in its claws, or like a bottle thrown into the sea. The point is: to be heard—even if by one single person.

François Mauriac

One goes on writing partly because it is the only available way of earning a living. It is a hard way and highly competitive. My heart drops into my bowels when I enter a bookshop and see how fierce the competition is. But one pushes on because one has to pay bills.

Anthony Burgess

One wants to tell a story, like Scheherazade, in order not to die. It's one of the oldest urges of mankind. It's a way of stalling death.

Carlos Fuentes

One writes to make a home for oneself, on paper, in time and in others' minds.

Alfred Kazin

Write to register history.

Isabel Allende

Curiosity urges you on—the driving force.

John Dos Passos

Despite all the cynical things writers have said about writing for money, the truth is we write for love. That is why it is so easy to exploit us. That is also why we pretend to be hard-boiled, saying things like "No man but a blockhead ever wrote except for money" (Samuel Johnson). Not true. No one but a blockhead ever wrote except for love. . . . You must do it for love. If you do it for money, no money will ever be enough, and eventually you will start imitating your first successes, straining hot water through the same old teabag. It doesn't work with tea, and it doesn't work with writing.

Erica Jong

It is the deepest desire of every writer, the one we never admit or even dare to speak of: to write a book we can leave as a legacy. And although it is sometimes easy to forget, wanting to be a writer is not about reviews or advances or how many copies are printed or sold. It is much simpler than that, and much more passionate. If you do it right, and if they publish it, you may actually leave something behind that can last forever.

Alice Hoffman

It is immoral not to tell.

Albert Camus

Words

Omit needless words. Vigorous writing is concise. A sentence should contain no unnecessary words, a paragraph no unnecessary sentences, for the same reason that a drawing should have no unnecessary lines and a machine no unnecessary parts. This requires not that the writer make all his sentences short, or that he avoid all detail and treat his subjects only in outline, but that every word tell.

William Strunk, Jr., AND **E. B. White**

There is always one right word; use it, despite its foul or merely ludicrous associations.

Dylan Thomas

The difference between the right word and the almost right word is the difference between lightning and the lightning bug.

Mark Twain

If you would be pungent, be brief; for it is with words as with sunbeams. The more they are condensed, the deeper they burn.

Robert Southey

The fewer the words used, the more concentrated the attention; and the greater the concentration, the greater the power.

David Lambuth

If it is possible to cut a word out, always cut it out.

George Orwell

The price of learning to use words is the development of an acute self-consciousness. Nor is it enough to pay attention to words only when you face the task of writing—that is like playing the violin only on the night of the concert. You must attend to words when you read, when you speak, when others speak. Words must become ever present in your waking life, an incessant concern, like color and design if the graphic arts matter to you, or pitch and rhythm if it is music, or speed and form if it is athletics.

Jacques Barzun

Words are to be taken seriously. I try to take seriously acts of language. Words set things in motion. I've seen them doing it. Words set up atmospheres, electrical fields, charges. I've felt them doing it. Words conjure. I try not to be careless about what I utter, write, sing. I'm careful about what I give voice to.

Toni Cade Bambara

....

Upon mature consideration I advise you to go no farther with your vocabulary. If you have a lot of words they will become like some muscle you have developed that you are compelled to use, and you must use this one in expressing yourself or in criticizing others. It is hard to say who will punish you the most for this, the dumb people who don't know what you are talking about or the learned ones who do. But wallop you they will and you will be forced to confine yourself to pen and paper.

Then you will be a writer and may God have mercy on your soul.

No! A thousand times no! Far, far better confine yourself to a few simple expressions in life, the ones that served billions upon countless billions of our fore-

fathers and still serve admirably all but a tiny handful of those at present clinging
to the earth's crust. . . .

So forget all that has hitherto attracted you in our complicated system of grunts
and go back to those fundamental ones that have stood the test of time.

F. Scott Fitzgerald,
IN A LETTER TO **Andrew Turnbull** (1932)

....

"The first law of writing," said Macaulay, "that law to which all
others are subordinate, is this: that the words employed shall be
such as to convey to the reader the meaning of the writer." Toward
that end, use familiar words—words that your readers will understand, and not words they will have to look up. No advice is more
elementary, and no advice is more difficult to accept. When we feel
an impulse to use a marvelously exotic word, let us lie down until
the impulse goes away.

James J. Kilpatrick

People don't like using dictionaries when they're reading mere
novels.

Anthony Burgess

Always look up words in a good dictionary, even when you know
what they mean.

Paul Scott

Good writing is all handmade. It's made of words. Looking up
words as you write is a vital step in research. A word choice isn't apt
merely because a word's formal definition seems to fit. Words are
layered with meaning, and the layers need to fit as well. If you write
"the final solution to our problem" unaware that "final solution"

translates the Nazi euphemism for the Holocaust, *die Endlösung;* if you write "a supercilious handshake" unaware that "supercilious" derives from Latin words meaning "above the eyelid" (i.e., with a lifted eyebrow), you communicate more and less to your reader than you intend. Sloppy word choice isn't only a literary sin; it's confusing. If you choose words with their multileveled meanings in mind, your reader will have a better chance of understanding what you mean—and so will you.

Richard Rhodes

You don't choose a word if you're a writer as a golf pro chooses a club with the *shot* in mind. You choose it with *yourself* in mind—*your* needs, *your* passions. It has to carry the green, yes, but it must also carry *you.*

Archibald MacLeish

A man who thinks much of his words as he writes them will generally leave behind him work that smells of oil.

Anthony Trollope

Words in prose ought to express the intended meaning; if they attract attention to themselves, it is a fault; in the very best styles you read page after page without noticing the medium.

Samuel Taylor Coleridge

Exercise your words. Try them out in new relationships.

William Sloane

Words have basic inalienable meanings, departure from which is either conscious metaphor or inexcusable vulgarity.

Evelyn Waugh

At a reading in 1968, the poet Marianne Moore solicited questions from the audience and someone asked, "What words of advice, if any, would you give to a beginning poet who hates words?" The 81-year-old Pulitzer Prize and National Book Award winner pondered for a moment and then replied, "That may be very auspicious. Words are a very great trap."

Words have weight, sound and appearance; it is only by considering these that you can write a sentence that is good to look at and good to listen to.

W. Somerset Maugham

Words, like eyeglasses, blur everything that they do not make more clear.

Joseph Joubert

Words: the pieces of change in the currency of a sentence. They must not get in the way. There is always too much small change.

Jules Renard

Word-carpentry is like any other kind of carpentry: you must join your sentences smoothly.

Anatole France

Words have to be crafted, not sprayed. They need to be fitted together with infinite care.

Norman Cousins

Short words are best and the old words when short are best of all.

Winston Churchill

The homely, concrete, Anglo-Saxon words in which we naturally think and speak are more effective in writing than the more abstract Latinisms.

David Lambuth

Don't use words too big for the subject. Don't say "infinitely" when you mean "very"; otherwise you'll have no word left when you want to talk about something *really* infinite.

C. S. Lewis

I never write *metropolis* for seven cents because I can get the same price for *city*. I never write *policeman* because I can get the same money for *cop*.

Mark Twain

A word once let out of the cage cannot be whistled back again.

Horace

Our words must seem to be inevitable.

William Butler Yeats

Writing is an affair of words rather than soul, impulse, "sincerity," or an instinct for the significant. If the words aren't there, nothing happens.

Paul Fussell

Psychoanalysts in France, structuralists in the United States and France, conservative, liberal and left-wing thinkers in contemporary schools of linguistic philosophy agree about one thing; man became man not by the tool but by the Word. It is not walking upright and using a stick to dig for food or strike a blow that makes a human being, it is speech. And neither intelligent apes nor dolphins whispering marvels in the ocean share with us the ability to transform this direct communication into the written word, which sets up an endless chain of communication and commune between peoples and generations who will never meet.

Nadine Gordimer

Work Habits

It is by sitting down to write every morning that one becomes a writer. Those who do not do this remain amateurs.

Gerald Brenan

You write by sitting down and writing. There's no particular time or place—you suit yourself, your nature. How one works, assuming he's disciplined, doesn't matter.

Bernard Malamud

Writers customarily write in the morning and try to make news, make love, or make friends in the afternoon.

Edward Hoagland

There comes a moment in the day, when you have written your pages in the morning, attended to your correspondence in the afternoon, and have nothing further to do. Then comes the hour when you are bored; that's the time for sex.

H. G. Wells

Get up very early and get going at once, in fact, work first and wash afterwards.

W. H. Auden

Don't work too hard. Fool around a bit. Be lazy. Don't worry, Life is—forever.

Henry Miller,

IN A LETTER TO **Lawrence Durrell** (1978)

It is helpful to write always at the same time of day. Scheduled obligations often raise problems, but an hour or two can almost always be found in the early morning—when the telephone never rings and no one knocks at the door. And it is important that you write something, regardless of quantity, every day. As the Romans put it, *Nulla dies sine linea*—No day without a line. (They were speaking of lines drawn by artists, but the rule applies as well to the writer.)

As a result of all this, the setting almost automatically evokes verbal behavior. No warm-up is needed. A circadian rhythm develops that is extremely powerful. At a certain time every day, you will be highly disposed to engage in serious verbal behavior.

B. F. Skinner

Write even when you don't want to, don't much like what you are writing, and aren't writing particularly well.

Agatha Christie

Now this is very important and can hardly be emphasized too strongly: *You have decided to write at four o'clock, and at four o'clock write you must!*

Dorothea Brande

My most important discovery has been that I have optimum hours for writing. These are between 10:00 A.M. and 2:00 P.M. For a lifetime I've told myself that I was a nighttime writer—it seemed romantic. But actually I'm tired at night, and that's when I prefer to read and research. Whatever your optimum hours are, *don't cheat yourself of them.* This is a daily battle. If you spend them answering the phone, attending to correspondence, etc., you'll find yourself empty-handed and out of sorts during your low tide.

Amy Wallace

BEST ADVICE on writing I've ever received: Finish.

Peter Mayle

Very few authors are able to do actual writing for more than three hours a day. In fact, a good many very successful ones average no more than an hour.

H. L. Mencken

It's a job. It's not a hobby. You don't write the way you build a model airplane. You have to sit down and work, to schedule your time and stick to it. Even if it's just for an hour or so each day, you have to get a babysitter and make the time. If you're going to make writing succeed you have to approach it as a job.

Rosellen Brown

THE BEST ADVICE on writing I've ever received is: Don't answer the phone.

Patsy Garlan

All this advice from senior writers to establish a discipline—always to get down a thousand words a day whatever one's mood—I find an absurdly puritanical and impractical approach. Write, if you must, because you feel like writing, never because you *ought* to write.

John Fowles

All good writing comes out of aloneness. You have to do it on an open highway. You wouldn't want to do it in New York City. But on Highway 40 West or some of those big open highways, you can hold the wheel with one hand and write with the other. It's a good discipline, because sometimes you can only write two or three words at a time before you have to look back at the road, so those three words have to count. The problem is whether you can read the damn thing by the time you reach your destination.

Sam Shepard

The best regimen is to get up early, insult yourself a bit in the shaving mirror, and then pretend you're cutting wood.

Lawrence Durrell

Writer's Block

If you are in difficulties with a book, try the element of surprise: attack it at an hour when it isn't expecting it.

H. G. Wells

When I have trouble writing, I step outside my studio into the garden and pull weeds until my mind clears—I find weeding to be the best therapy there is for writer's block.

Irving Stone

I've never been blocked, but there are times when the words won't come. When I feel dried-up I deal myself a few games of solitaire at my desk. I've been doing it all my life. Sometimes I play 10 or 20 games, sometimes 40. Once, I played for three straight days. The important thing is not to leave the work place.

Richard Condon

Sometimes when I'm stuck I go to an office building, ride the elevator and stare at the lawyers, stock brokers, and accountants in their power suits. Just the thought of having to wear pantyhose all day and work in a building where I can't open the windows usually makes me grateful to come home and write. If that doesn't work, I forbid myself to write for a week. The subconscious doesn't like being told what to do and it frequently becomes inventive after an enforced vacation. Other times, I put aside what I'm blocked on and work on something else. Shopping, of course, helps.

Margo Kaufman

Never rely on shopping as a cure for writer's block and/or depression. It's not a good escape but a trap that clutters up your life with possessions that require attention and care.

Janet AND **Isaac Asimov**

Eat massive amounts of high-calorie food. It won't get you writing, but now you'll have bathos knocked.

Alice Kahn

If you're afraid you can't write, the answer is to write. Every sentence you construct adds weight to the balance pan. If you're afraid of what other people will think of your efforts, don't show them until you write your way beyond your fear. If writing a book is impossible, write a chapter. If writing a chapter is impossible, write a page. If writing a page is impossible, write a paragraph. If writing a paragraph is impossible, write a sentence. If writing even a sentence is impossible, write a word and teach yourself everything there is to know about that word and then write another, connected word and see where their connection leads. A page a day is a book a year.

Richard Rhodes

The best thing is to write anything, anything at all that comes into your head, until gradually there is a calm and creative day.

Stephen Spender

Copy out the first thirty pages of an obscure 19th century French novel and then carry on with your own text. Later, go back and rewrite the first thirty pages. Tolstoy tried this with *Anna Karenina* and it worked.

Andrew Cockburn

I think the best thing any writer can do is keep a journal. If you write on a computer, you should keep your journal on the computer. During writer's block, your journal is invaluable. Write to yourself about being blocked. Explain to yourself the feelings of frustration you are feeling, or the anger you are having with your talent for letting you down. Describe to yourself the chapter or scene you are writing: who the characters are and where you are trying to get to in the chapter or scene. Write about it. Believe me, it will start to come, right there in your journal.

Dominick Dunne

When I sit down in order to write, sometimes it's there; sometimes it's not. But that doesn't bother me anymore. I tell my students there is such a thing as "writer's block," and they should respect it. You shouldn't write through it. It's blocked because it ought to be blocked, because you haven't got it right now.

Toni Morrison

My prescription for writer's block is to face the fact that there is no such thing. It's an invented condition, a literary version of the judicial "abuse excuse." Writing *well* is difficult, but one can always write *something*. And then, with a lot of work, make it better. It's a question of having enough will and ambition, not of hoping to evade this mysterious hysteria people are always talking about.

Thomas Mallon

My prescription for writer's block? Alimony—the world's greatest muse.

Dick Schaap

Pretend you're taking up a new profession, like plumbing.

Whitney Balliett

Turn on any Puccini opera.

Ken Auletta

Report. Writers are less interesting than they think. Fortunately, the rest of the world is more interesting. Interview people. Look at things. Don't just sit at the computer.

Jeffrey Toobin

I don't think that writer's block exists really. I think that when you're trying to do something prematurely, it just won't come. Certain subjects just need time. . . . You've got to wait before you write about them.

Joyce Carol Oates

Writer's block is a luxury most people with deadlines don't have.

Diane Ackerman

Sit in sun. Sun goes behind cloud. Look at watch. Notice that second-hand does not always point directly at little marks on dial. Sometimes it does, though. Then sometimes it doesn't. Why? Feel panic at how quickly life slips by. Get to work.

Nicholson Baker

Put the paper in the typewriter, stare at it a long time, get snow-blindness if you have to, but write something.

Erma Bombeck

The prescription is prevention: keep working, cross your fingers, get plenty of fresh air.

Kurt Andersen

My prescription for writer's block: Write badly. Bad writing is easier. And it must be popular, there's so much of it.

P. J. O'Rourke

Writer's block, how to overcome it: write something substantial every morning, and while doing so forget entirely the impression you're creating. That is, overcome ego.

Paul Fussell

Ignore it: you never stop speaking; why stop writing?

Quentin Crisp

Don't concede it exists.

Richard Ford

[Writer's block] doesn't exist. Stay at your desk and something always occurs to you.

Patrick McGrath

The cure is similar to that of lycanthropy: to know that there is no such thing.

Nick Tosches

Walk around the block.

Bob Colacello

Be alone
Till you're in the zone.

Patsy Garlan

The successful writer listens to himself. You get a writer's block by being aware that you're putting it out there.

Frank Herbert

I THINK the best advice on writing I've received was from John Steinbeck, who suggested that one way to get around writer's block (which I was suffering hideously at the time) was to pretend to be writing to an aunt, or a girl friend. I did this, writing to an actress friend I knew, Jean Seberg. The editors of *Harper's* forgot to take off the salutation and that's how the article begins in the magazine: *Dear Jean . . .*

George Plimpton

The professional guts a book through . . . in full knowledge that what he is doing is not very good. Not to work is to exhibit a failure of nerve, and a failure of nerve is the best definition I know for writer's block.

John Gregory Dunne

The idea is to get the pencil moving quickly.

Bernard Malamud

Sit there until the screen is full. Get up. Return and edit what's on the screen. Having something to delete is better than a blank screen.

Margaret Carlson

Take five ice cubes, place in clean glass, add vodka.

Actually, I've found that writer's block occurs most frequently at the very top of one's work. So lose that tortured lead you were laboring over—it probably wasn't any good, anyway—and write it straight. Halfway through the piece it'll come to you—and it'll better rhyme with what you were after when you began.

Phil Mushnick

Any writer who has difficulty in writing is probably not onto his true subject, but wasting time with false, petty goals; as soon as you connect with your true subject you will write.

Joyce Carol Oates

Force yourself to write non-stop for twenty or thirty minutes: no deletions, no erasures, no pauses. If that doesn't work, take a break. Take a walk. Pack up your writing supplies and go someplace new. Sit in a coffee shop, find a cozy spot in a library, go to a park. If you're truly desperate, go away for a few days. Take a train to a distant city and write onboard (on Amtrak, you can actually plug in your computer. But coffee is essential: without it, the train will rock you to sleep). It often helps to do something entirely nonverbal, like making a collage or playing music. And it always helps to understand that writer's block is a widespread malady. To strengthen your feeling of solidarity with the scribbling classes, rent these movies: *The Shining, Misery, Barton Fink, Deconstructing Harry,* all of which explore the consequences of writer's block.

Nancy Hathaway

It is often said that reading, for writers, is a busman's holiday. This is true, but I have found it to be one of the best cures for writer's block. Reading certain authors—Nabokov, for example—makes me feel jealous and tired. Reading Robert Aickman, my favorite short-story writer, invariably makes me want to pick up my pen. One type of genius hampers me, while another inspires.

My greatest pleasure is reading ghost and horror stories. I have read thousands. Occasionally I stumble on a really superb tale, and it makes me want to write like nothing else. If you can find writing that makes you feel this way, use it.

Amy Wallace

Prescription for writer's block: fear of poverty.

Peter Mayle

There is no cure for writer's block. If it persists into the third day the writer must abandon all hope of authorship and go into the family business. Those who refuse this common sense alternative should identify the source of the block. When it is the result of fear the writer must complete the work and submit it even if humiliation and death are sure to follow. When it is the result of visceral disinterest, which sometimes emerges after agreeing to write something or other, it is better to own up frankly and abandon the work.

Thomas Powers

I heard some writer say that his "father was a truck driver, and you know what, never in his life did that man get truck driver's block."

Barnaby Conrad

It would be wisest not to worry too much about the sterile periods. They ventilate the subject and instill into it the reality of daily life.

André Gide

Sometimes the "block" is a good thing. Yes, we're stalled from the process of producing words, but perhaps we are not ready to write at our best, and an inner voice (the "block") is telling us that, and holding us back . . . and perhaps doing us a favor until we're ready to produce what's truly worthy of us. Too often writers write too much. They do not know the good from their inferior work, and their publishers release whatever the writer hands in *if* the writer has a "name." There is no way to lose a "name" faster than to produce again and again unworthy work, and maybe it would be better for their reputations if they'd been "blocked" from doing so much bad writing.

Gay Talese

Prescription for writer's block: Begin. (With a pen, not a machine.)

Cynthia Ozick

Move to New York City. Get married. Buy an incredibly expensive apartment. Have children, a dog, a second home in the country. Lease an imported luxury automobile. Come the first of the month, I promise, you will have no problem writing.

Bruce Feirstein

When I hear about writer's block, this one and that one! Fuck off! Stop writing, for Christ's sake: You're not meant to be doing this. Plenty more where you came from.

Gore Vidal

The Writer's Life

Be regular and orderly like a bourgeois, so that you may be violent and original in your work.

Gustave Flaubert

I am a writer who came of a sheltered life. A sheltered life can be a daring life as well. For all serious daring starts from within.

Eudora Welty

A NOVELIST FRIEND years ago gave me two pieces of sage advice— (1) never fuck a fan and (2) never engage in an argument with a correspondent.

John Gregory Dunne

It is hard to master both life and work equally well. So if you are bound to fake one of them, it had better be life.

Joseph Brodsky

A writer's life is not designed to reassure your mother.

Rita Mae Brown

....

I'm sorry you had an argument with your father. But from where I sit, and I sit a little bit along the road you are travelling, you have only one thing in the world to do. You must *finish* this book and then you must *finish* another. If anything at all, saving your own death, stops you, except momentarily, then you are not a writer anyway and there is nothing to discuss. I do not mean that you should not bitch and complain and fight and scrabble but the one important thing for you is to get your work done. If anyone gets hurt in the process, you cannot be blamed.

But don't think for a moment that you will ever be forgiven for being what they call "different." You won't! I still have not been forgiven. Only when I am delivered in a pine box will I be considered "safe." After I had written the Grapes of Wrath and it had been to a large extent read and sometimes burned, the librarians at Salinas Public Library, who had known my folks, remarked that it was lucky my parents were dead so that they did not have to suffer this shame. I tell you this so you may know what to expect.

Now get to work—

John Steinbeck,
IN A LETTER TO **Dennis Murphy** (1956)

....

It is not a good thing for an artist to marry. As the ancients used to say, if you serve a Muse, you must serve her and no one else. An unhappy marriage may perhaps contribute to the development of talent, but a happy one is no good at all.

Ivan Turgenev

The greatest service a wife can render her writer husband is not typing his manuscripts for him, but keeping people away from him. Of course, a husband might do the same, if his wife is the writer.

Patricia Highsmith

THE BEST ADVICE on writing I've ever received: "Don't have children." I gave it to myself.

Richard Ford

Someone once asked me whether I thought women artists should have children, and, since we were beyond discussing why this question is never asked of artists who are men, I gave my answer promptly.

"Yes," I said, somewhat to my surprise. And, as if to amend my rashness, I added: "They should have children—*assuming this is of interest to them*—but only one."

"Why only one?" this Someone wanted to know.

"Because with one you can move," I said. "With more than one you're a sitting duck."

Alice Walker

Always be nice to those younger than you, because they are the ones who will be writing about you.

Cyril Connolly

Keep your bones in good motion, kid, and quietly consume and digest what is necessary. I think it is not so much important to build a literary thing as it is not to hurt things. I think it is important to be quiet and in love with park benches; solve whole areas of pain by walking across a rug.

Charles Bukowski,
IN A LETTER TO **John William Corrington** (1963)

Writing Advice

Nobody can advise and help you, nobody. There is only one single means. Go inside yourself. Discover the motive that bids you write; examine whether it sends its roots down to the deepest places of your heart, confess to yourself whether you would have to die if writing were denied you. This before all: ask yourself in the quietest hour of your night: *must* I write?

Rainer Maria Rilke

My experience with trying to help people to write has been limited but extremely intensive. I have done everything from giving would-be writers money to live on to plotting and rewriting their stories for them, and so far I have found it all to be a waste. The people whom God or nature intended to be writers find their own answers, and those who have to ask are impossible to help. They are merely people who want to be writers.

Raymond Chandler

My father, Irving Wallace, was very fond of giving writerly advice. He was also quite superstitious about his writing habits. He would never use any typewriter besides the one he'd been given at the age of 16 (he used it for 57 years), and he would only use one type of pencil for making corrections: Blackwings. (Blackwings have a little motto on the side: "Half the pressure, twice the speed." I pondered over this koan for decades.)

The following is a list, in no particular order, of some of his thoughts:

1. Don't wait for inspiration to strike. Write every day. Get the whole book down, no matter how bad the first draft may seem. Worry about polishing afterwards.

2. Don't tell your stories before they are written. If you do, you will get your "reward" in advance—the listener's delight and fascination. This can prevent you from ever telling your story on paper.

3. Prepare your research thoroughly. Outline, knowing that you will inevitably change it.

4. If you are writing non-fiction, it's okay to sell the idea based on an outline or a few chapters, in order to get an advance and have a deadline. If you can afford it, *do not* do this with fiction. It's very dangerous—you will present an idea to an editor, and they will develop an idea of the novel, while you are finding that you want to change it. They may feel cheated by the finished product.

5. If your career is taking off and you are offered a multiple-book deal, resist it if you possibly can. Financial need may prevent this, but it can be entrapping.

6. Leave something in your book for the editor to take out. (Irving very slyly tricked his editor at Simon & Schuster, Michael Korda, for 25 years. When Michael

wanted Irving to trim down a book, he'd always offer up something to be cut while making it appear that he was making a sacrifice.)

7. Irving used to tell me bedtime stories that were real cliff-hangers. He liked to leave me asking, "What happened next?" He said the reader should always have that feeling when ending a chapter of a book.

8. When you get bad reviews, calm yourself by remembering what somebody famous once said: "Critics are legless runners."

9. If you get 10 rejections for a story or article in the mail, send out 20 more submissions that day. Have the envelopes ready.

10. It's okay to marry another writer, but never marry an actor. (Irving worked as a screenwriter in Hollywood for many years.)

11. People are marvelously blind about whether they have been used as characters in your stories, so be artful but don't worry too much about being caught. Irving told me once about using an acquaintance of his as the model for a character in his first best-seller, *The Chapman Report*. Apparently she was a nymphomaniac who had slept with the entire UCLA orchestra. When the book came out, there was a party to honor its publication, and she and her husband attended. Irving began to sweat bullets when she approached him and insisted that they talk. She said, "Irving, I loved *The Chapman Report*, but when are you going to put *me* in one of your books?!"

> 12. Never, ever get involved in the making of your books
> into movies. My father told me that Irving Stone once
> said to him, "I've had the ideal situation: all my books
> have been optioned for movies, but none of them
> have been made."
>
> **Amy Wallace**

Often I am asked if any writer ever helped or advised me. None
did. However, I was not asking for help either, and I do not believe
one should. If one wishes to write, he or she had better be writing,
and there is no real way in which one writer can help another. Each
must find his own way.

Louis L'Amour

The "best advice" I think is in *reading* good writers, not seeking advice from them, for we learn best by emulating the best.

Gay Talese

There is no advice to give young poets.

Pablo Neruda

Don't ever write anything you don't like yourself and if you do like
it, don't take anyone else's advice about changing it. They just don't
know.

Raymond Chandler

I never presume to give advice on writing. I think the best way to
learn to write is to read books and stories by good writers. It's a

hard thing to preach about. As Thelonious Monk once said, about his field, "Talking about music is like dancing about architecture."

Maureen Dowd

If I had to give young writers advice, I'd say don't listen to writers talking about writing or themselves.

Lillian Hellman

IN THE AFTERNOONS, Gertrude Stein and I used to go antique hunting in the local shops, and I remember once asking her if she thought I should become a writer. In the typically cryptic way we were all so enchanted with, she said, "No." I took that to mean yes and sailed for Italy the next day.

Woody Allen

Selected Bibliography

Anthologies

Bolker, Joan, ed. *The Writer's Home Companion*. New York: Henry Holt, 1997.

Brohaugh, William, ed. *Just Open a Vein*. Cincinnati: Writer's Digest Books, 1987.

Burack, A. S., ed. *The Writer's Handbook*. Boston: The Writer, 1980.

Burack, Sylvia K., ed. *The Writer's Handbook*. Boston: The Writer, 1997.

Edgarian, Carol, and Tom Jenks, eds. *The Writer's Life*. New York: Vintage, 1997.

Heffron, Jack, ed. *The Best Writing on Writing*. 2 vols. Cincinnati: Story Press, 1994–95.

National Book Award Authors. *The Writing Life*. New York: Random House, 1995.

Zinsser, William, ed. *Inventing the Truth*. Boston: Houghton Mifflin, 1987.

Craft

Algren, Nelson. *Nonconformity: Writing on Writing*. New York: Seven Stories Press, 1996.

Asimov, Isaac, and Janet Asimov. *How to Enjoy Writing*. New York: Walker, 1987.

Atchity, Kenneth. *A Writer's Time*. New York: Norton, 1986.

Barnes, Julian. *Flaubert's Parrot*. New York: Vintage, 1990.

Barzun, Jacques. *On Writing, Editing, and Publishing*. Chicago: University of Chicago Press, 1971.

Bradbury, Ray. *Zen in the Art of Writing*. Santa Barbara: Capra Press, 1989.

Brande, Dorothea. *Becoming a Writer*. Los Angeles: J. P. Tarcher, 1981.

Brown, Rita Mae. *Starting from Scratch*. New York: Bantam, 1988.

Burnett, Hallie. *On Writing the Short Story.* New York: Harper & Row, 1983.

Burnham, Sophy. *For Writers Only.* New York: Ballantine, 1994.

Dillard, Annie. *Living by Fiction.* New York: Harper Colophon, 1983.

Elbow, Peter. *Writing with Power.* New York: Oxford, 1981.

Feuss, Billings S. *How to Use the Power of the Printed Word.* New York: Anchor, 1985.

Gardner, John. *The Art of Fiction.* New York: Knopf, 1983.

———. *On Becoming a Novelist.* New York: Harper & Row, 1983.

Goldberg, Natalie. *Wild Mind: Living the Writer's Life.* New York: Bantam, 1990.

———. *Writing Down the Bones.* Boston: Shambhala, 1986.

Goldman, William. *Adventures in the Screen Trade.* New York: Warner, 1983.

Higgins, George V. *On Writing.* New York: Henry Holt, 1990.

Hills, Rust. *Writing in General and the Short Story in Particular.* New York: Bantam, 1979.

Krull, Kathleen. *Twelve Keys to Writing Books That Sell.* Cincinnati: Writer's Digest Books, 1989.

Lamott, Anne. *Bird by Bird.* New York: Pantheon, 1994.

Mamet, David. *Writing in Restaurants.* New York: Penguin, 1987.

Maugham, W. Somerset. *The Summing Up.* New York: Penguin, 1963.

Rhodes, Richard. *How to Write.* New York: Morrow, 1995.

Rilke, Rainer Maria. *Letters to a Young Poet.* Translated by Joan M. Burnham. San Rafael, Calif.: New World Library, 1992.

Scott, Paul. *On Writing and the Novel.* New York: Morrow, 1987.

Sloane, William. *The Craft of Writing.* New York: Norton, 1983.

Ueland, Brenda. *If You Want to Write.* St. Paul: Graywolf, 1987.

Vargas Llosa, Mario. *A Writer's Reality.* Boston: Houghton Mifflin, 1991.

Zinsser, William. *On Writing Well.* 2nd. ed. New York: Harper & Row, 1980.

Editing and Publishing

Adler, Bill. *Inside Publishing.* New York: Bobbs-Merrill, 1982.

Appelbaum, Judith. *How to Get Happily Published.* 4th ed. New York: HarperCollins, 1992.

Boswell, John. *The Awful Truth About Publishing*. New York: Warner, 1986.

Curtis, Richard. *Beyond the Bestseller*. New York: New American Library, 1989.

Gross, Gerald, ed. *Editors on Editing*. 3rd ed. New York: Grove, 1993.

Henderson, Bill, ed. *The Art of Literary Publishing*. Wainscott, N.Y.: Pushcart Press, 1995.

Grammar and Usage

Bernstein, Theodore M. *The Careful Writer*. New York: Atheneum, 1977.

Flesch, Rudolf. *Say What You Mean*. New York: Harper & Row, 1972.

Gowers, Ernest. *The Complete Plain Words*. Boston: David R. Godine, 1988.

Graves, Robert, and Alan Hodge. *The Reader over Your Shoulder*. 2nd ed. New York: Vintage, 1979.

Kilpatrick, James J. *The Writer's Art*. Kansas City, Mo.: Andrews, McMeel & Parker, 1984.

Lambuth, David. *The Golden Book on Writing*. New York: Penguin, 1976.

Safire, William. *Fumblerules*. New York: Doubleday, 1990.

Strunk, William, Jr., and E. B. White. *The Elements of Style*. 3rd ed. New York: Macmillan, 1979.

Interviews

Lamb, Brian, ed. *Booknotes*. New York: Times Books, 1997.

Odier, Daniel, ed. *The Job: Interviews with William S. Burroughs*. New York: Grove, 1974.

Plimpton, George, ed. *Writers at Work: The Paris Review Interviews*. Series 1–9. New York: Viking Penguin, 1957–92.

Letters

Asimov, Stanley, ed. *Yours, Isaac Asimov*. New York: Doubleday, 1987.

Baker, Carlos, ed. *Ernest Hemingway: Selected Letters*. New York: Scribner, 1981.

Blotner, Joseph, ed. *Selected Letters of William Faulkner*. New York: Vintage, 1978.

Charters, Ann, ed. *Jack Kerouac: Selected Letters, 1940–1956*. New York: Viking Penguin, 1995.

Cheever, Benjamin, ed. *The Letters of John Cheever*, New York: Simon & Schuster, 1989.

Cooney, Seamus, ed. *Charles Bukowski: Screams from the Balcony: Selected Letters, 1960–1970*. Santa Rosa: Black Sparrow Press, 1993.

Forgue, Guy J., ed. *Letters of H. L. Mencken*. Boston: Northeastern University Press, 1981.

MacNiven, Ian S., ed. *The Durrell-Miller Letters, 1935–1980*. New York: New Directions, 1988.

McShane, Frank, ed. *Selected Letters of Raymond Chandler*. New York: Dell, 1987.

Rogers, Marion Elizabeth, ed. *Mencken & Sara: A Life in Letters*. New York: McGraw-Hill, 1987.

Steinbeck, Elaine, and Robert Wallsten, eds. *Steinbeck: A Life in Letters*. New York: Viking Penguin, 1975.

Turnbull, Andrew, ed. *The Letters of F. Scott Fitzgerald*. New York: Scribner, 1963.

Wheelock, John Hall, ed. *Editor to Author: The Letters of Maxwell E. Perkins*. New York, Scribners, 1950.

Memoirs

Baker, Russell, *Growing Up*. New York: Signet, 1984.

Bennett, Alan. *Writing Home*. New York: Random House, 1994.

Cheever, John. *The Journals of John Cheever*. New York: Knopf, 1991.

Dunne, John Gregory. *Harp*. New York: Simon & Schuster, 1989.

Hall, Donald. *Remembering Poets*. New York: Harper Colophon, 1978.

King, Larry L. *None but a Blockhead*. New York: Viking, 1986.

Mitford, Jessica. *Poison Penmanship: The Gentle Art of Muckraking*. New York: Knopf, 1979.

Saroyan, William. *After Thirty Years: The Daring Young Man on the Flying Trapeze*. New York: Harcourt, Brace & World, 1964.

Vonnegut, Kurt. *Fates Worse Than Death.* New York: Putnam, 1991.

Welty, Eudora. *One Writer's Beginnings.* Cambridge: Harvard University Press, 1983.

Periodicals

The Paris Review
Publisher's Weekly
Writer's Digest

Quotations

Brennan, Thomas H., ed. *Writings on Writing.* Jefferson, N.C.: McFarland & Co., 1994.

Murray, Donald M., ed. *Shoptalk.* Portsmouth, N.H.: Boynton/Cook Publishers, 1990.

Phillips, Larry W., ed. *Ernest Hemingway on Writing.* New York: Scribner, 1983.

———, ed. *F. Scott Fitzgerald on Writing.* New York: Scribner, 1985.

Plimpton, George, ed. *The Writer's Chapbook.* New York: Viking Penguin, 1989.

Safire, William, and Leonard Safir, eds. *Good Advice on Writing.* New York: Simon & Schuster, 1992.

Winokur, Jon. *Writers on Writing,* 2nd ed. Philadelphia: Running Press, 1987.

Permissions Acknowledgments

Grateful acknowledgment is made to the following for permission to reprint previously published and new material:

Jeffrey Carver: "Advice to Aspiring Writers" by Jeffrey Carver, copyright © 1998 by Jeffrey Carver. Reprinted by permission of the author.

Harlan Ellison: Excerpted material on writing and the writer by Harlan Ellison, copyright © 1999 by The Kilimanjaro Corporation. All rights reserved. Reprinted by permission of the author.

International Creative Management, Inc.: Excerpt from *What Men Don't Tell Women* by Roy Blount, Jr. (First published in *Reader's Digest*), copyright © 1984 by Roy Blount, Jr. Reprinted by permission of International Creative Management, Inc.

Florence King: "How to Handle an Incompetent Copy Editor" by Florence King, copyright © 1999 by Florence King. Reprinted by permission of the author.

William Morrow & Company: Excerpts from *How to Write* by Richard Rhodes, copyright © 1995 by Richard Rhodes. Reprinted by permission of William Morrow & Company.

Random House, Inc.: Excerpt from "Upon Receiving the Nobel Prize for Literature" from *Essays, Speeches & Public Letters by Faulkner* by William Faulkner, edited by James B. Meriwether, copyright © 1950 by William Faulkner. Reprinted by permission of Random House, Inc.

Simon & Schuster and The Wylie Agency, Inc.: John Cheever's letter to John Weaver from *The Letters of John Cheever* by Benjamin Cheever, copyright © 1988 by Benjamin Cheever. Reprinted by permission of Simon & Schuster and The Wylie Agency, Inc. No changes shall be made to the text of this work without the express written consent of The Wylie Agency, Inc.

Index

Auletta, Ken:
  on editors, 39
  on the reader, 134
  on writer's block, 193

Babel, Isaak, on simile, 79
Bainbridge, Beryl, on the secret, 154
Baker, Nicholson:
  on editors and editing, 37
  on plagiarism, 94
  on writer's block, 193
Baker, Russell:
  on characters, 8–9
  on punctuation, 120
Baker, Sheridan, on metaphor, 157
Baldwin, James:
  on style, 159–60
  on why you write, 176
Balliett, Whitney:
  on editors, 34
  on tricks of the trade, 170
  on writer's block, 193
Bambara, Toni Cade:
  on the short story, 57
  on words, 180
Bamberger, Michael, on sports
    writing, 67
Banks, Russell:
  on agents, 4
  on editors and editing, 34
  on reading, 140
Barnes, Julian, on discouragement,
    26
Barry, Dave:
  on book tours, 112
  on editors, 40
  on humor writing, 65
Barthelme, Donald, on material, 85
Barzun, Jacques:
  on encouragement, 45
  on process, 104
  on words, 180

Baudelaire, Charles, on style, 161
Beattie, Ann, on characters, 11
Beckett, Samuel, on encouragement,
    52
Bell, Madison Smartt, on drink, 31
Bellow, Saul:
  on characters, 10
  on process, 108
  on the secret, 154
Benchley, Robert:
  on plagiarism, 95
  on style, 158
Bennett, Alan, on theatre versus
    television, 70–71
Berkow, Ira, on journalism, 66, 67
Bernays, Anne, on style, 160
Bernstein, Theodore M.:
  on allegory, 72–73
  on grammar and usage, 78
Berryman, John, on criticism, 16
Blount, Roy, Jr.:
  on occupational hazards, 91–92
  on publicity and promotion, 111
Boggess, Louise, on magazine
    articles, 68
Bombeck, Erma, on writer's block,
    194
Boswell, John:
  on agents, 3
  on publishers and publishing,
    118, 119
Boswell, Thomas, on sports writing,
    67
Bourjaily, Vance, on material, 83
Bova, Ben:
  on science fiction, 62
  on tricks of the trade, 174
Bowen, Catherine Drinker:
  on biography, 63–64
  on qualifications and
    requirements, 129
Bowen, Elizabeth, on dialogue, 20

About the Editor

JON WINOKUR is the author of various books, including *The Portable Curmudgeon, Zen to Go, The Rich Are Different,* and *Je Ne Sais* What? He lives in Pacific Palisades, California.